PENGUIN BOOKS

THE LAST DAYS OF HAUTE CUISINE

Patric Kuh is a Paris-trained chef who has worked in preeminent restaurants in France, New York, and California. He has written for *Gourmet*, *Esquire*, and *Food and Wine*, and is the restaurant critic for *Los Angeles Magazine*. He is the author of a novel, *An Available Man*. He lives in Los Angeles, California.

Praise for *The Last Days of Haute Cuisine*

"As an author, food writer and Paris-trained chef, Mr. Kuh plies his combined trades for an insider's tour of haute cuisine. . . . it is a luscious journey. *Haute Cuisine* is a well-crafted, engaging, informative and, at times, laugh-out-loud treatise on how we came to care about good food and the colorful characters who shaped our concept of what good food is."
—*The Dallas Morning News*

"Like a busy kitchen, Kuh's book has a lot going on . . . the thematic ingredients come together to produce a stimulating, satisfying and memorable experience."
—*Los Angeles Times*

"In *The Last Days of Haute Cuisine* gastronome Patric Kuh serves up the tale of America's culinary revolution, a ripe and intoxicating coulis of history, humor and dish."
—*Vanity Fair*

"In this fascinating study, Kuh traces the dramatic change in upscale American restaurants that took place in the last half of the twentieth century."   —*Newsday*

"*The Last Days of Haute Cuisine* is delicious reading. Kuh is a witty, knowledgeable, resourceful writer—and agreeably irreverent as well."   —*The Washington Post*

"Kuh not only writes well—you will find elegant passages throughout the book—he adroitly ties together his themes and his cast of characters."   —*Chicago Tribune*

"*The Last Days of Haute Cuisine* is a breezy history of American high-end restaurants . . . rollicking."
—*The New Yorker*

THE LAST
DAYS OF
HAUTE
CUISINE

PATRIC KUH

Penguin Books

PENGUIN BOOKS

Published by the Penguin Group
Penguin Putnam Inc., 375 Hudson Street, New York, New York 10014, U.S.A.
Penguin Books Ltd, 80 Strand, London WC2R 0RL, England
Penguin Books Australia Ltd, 250 Camberwell Road,
Camberwell, Victoria 3124, Australia
Penguin Books Canada Ltd, 10 Alcorn Avenue, Toronto, Ontario, Canada M4V 3B2
Penguin Books India (P) Ltd, 11 Community Centre,
Panchsheel Park, New Delhi – 110 017, India
Penguin Books (N.Z.) Ltd, Cnr Rosedale and Airborne Roads,
Albany, Auckland, New Zealand
Penguin Books (South Africa) (Pty) Ltd, 24 Sturdee Avenue,
Rosebank, Johannesburg 2196, South Africa

Penguin Books Ltd, Registered Offices: Harmondsworth, Middlesex, England

First published in the United States of America by Viking Penguin,
a member of Penguin Putnam Inc. 2001
Published in Penguin Books 2002

1 3 5 7 9 10 8 6 4 2

Grateful acknowledgment is made for permission to reprint
excerpts from the following copyrighted works:
Avis DeVoto papers, Schlesinger Library, Radcliffe Institute, Harvard University.
Love and Kisses and a Halo of Truffles by John Ferrone. Copyright © 1994 by John Ferrone.
Reprinted by permission of Arcade Publishing, New York, New York.
Obituary of Henry Soulé, *The New York Times*, January 29, 1966. Copyright © 1966 by
The New York Times Company. By permission of The New York Times.

THE LIBRARY OF CONGRESS HAS CATALOGED THE HARDCOVER EDITION AS FOLLOWS:
Kuh, Patric, 1964–
The last days of haute cuisine / Patric Kuh.
p.   cm.
ISBN 0-670-89178-9 (hc.)
ISBN 0 14 20.0031 0 (pbk.)
1. Restaurants—United States—History—20th century.
2. Gastronomy—History—20th century.   I. Title.
TX945.K79 2001
647.9573'09'04—dc21   00-042884

Printed in the United States of America
Set in Aries with Sackers Light Classic and Rococo Ornaments
Designed by Carla Bolte

FOR BONNIE

ACKNOWLEDGMENTS

The difficulty in writing about decades one has not known is how to make the time real. While published sources were an invaluable help to me, the detail that brought those earlier decades to life invariably came from the recollections of people who had lived through them. For facilitating my access to several of those individuals, I thank Fern Berman, Kathleen Duffy, Cristina Salas-Porras, and Bridget Watkins. For their generosity with their time—and their recollections—I am greatly indebted to the following: Michael Aaron, the late Joe Baum, Willy Bishop, Jerry Brody, Ed Giobbi, Barbara Kafka, George Lang, Maurice Lartigau, Sirio Maccioni, Michael McCarty, Richard Melman, Danny Meyer, Drew Nieporent, Bradley Ogden, the late Richard Olney, Pierre Orsi, Jacques Pépin, Mark Peel, Frank Prial, Michael Romano, Nancy Silverton, Abdallah Simon, André Soltner, André Surmain, Jeremiah Tower, Patricia Unterman, Jean Vergnes, Alice Waters, and Michael Whiteman.

I have been fortunate to have as friends two chefs, Alain Giraud and Gerald Hirigoyen, who helped me to understand the many subtleties of *la bonne table*. I am grateful to my editor, Ray Roberts, for urging me to keep on writing when the task of making it real seemed overwhelming. I am particularly grateful to Darrell Corti, who in addition to his generosity with his own archival material, one day in Sacramento put a copy of Delmonico's chef Charles Ranhofer's tome *The Epicurean* before me, flipped it to the recipe for "Cream of Green Corn à la Mendocino," and brought me to what would be one of the great switching points in American gastronomy. Finally, I owe a special debt of gratitude to Roger Fessaguet. Not only has his help been continuous throughout the writing of this book, but, in addition, while talking one day in Maine, he leaped from his seat, shot imaginary cuffs, hovered, beaming, as if he were about to perform some tableside carving, and by conjuring up the image of Henri Soulé so realistically before me gave me the necessary encouragement to try and make him real myself.

CONTENTS

CHARCOAL-BROILED

FLAMBÉED

GRILLED

WOOD-FIRED

THE LAST DAYS OF
HAUTE CUISINE

INTRODUCTION

In the restaurant business, there are no tomorrows. It is always right here, right now, this service, this meal. Make a mistake today and tomorrow your customers are eating somewhere else. Joe Baum, being the ultimate restaurateur, didn't want to talk about what he'd done but about what he was doing. We were sitting at the bar of the Rainbow Room in Rockefeller Center. I sipped a quartz-clear martini, he drank mineral water. I asked about the Newarker, at which he'd first made his mark in 1953. He parried with what he was doing at Windows on the World in 1997. I asked about his starting the Four Seasons in 1959. He came back with how well business was going at the Rainbow Room. Finally, he relented. "Ah, the 1950s," he said, and he cracked a devilish grin. It was as if he were saying, "You have no idea how different it was."

How different? It was literally a different country. Men wore gray-flannel suits. Women wore hats. Going out to dinner in America was still a very special occasion. But everyday American life was about to be transformed by the intersecting vectors of affluence and opportunity, and perhaps none more so than our relationship to restaurants. The Edwardian ideal of the grand hotel dining room with chandeliers and potted palms was over, the age when national

1

cuisines were broken down to their component microclimates not yet begun. In 1950, we didn't have to choose between Northern and Southern Italian, Asian fusion, Cal-Med, Ital-Med, or Franco-Californian. Contemplating a meal at a certain price range, we had one very simple decision to make. Did we want to sit among drapes of red velvet or in a cocoon of red leatherette?

The material defined the sort of food we could expect to be served. In the restaurant with the red leatherette booths, there was a certain American frankness. The Delmonico club steak would be charred, the creamed spinach made fresh, the Idaho potato really baked (and not steamed for easier reheating), the martinis that were consumed throughout the meal were served "up" and bone-dry. While the barroom at "21" defined the style, every major American city had its version. In Boston, it was Dinty Moore's; in Chicago, the Sirloin Room at the Stockyard Inn; in San Francisco, it was Jack's; and in Los Angeles, Chasen's. We felt comfortable in these restaurants. The barman mixing the drinks behind the bar was a welcoming presence. The menu was in English. The dark wainscoting gave the rooms a familiar warmth. What we didn't feel was sophisticated here. Not in the European sense. For that we had to choose the red velvet option.

Into these restaurants we walked with clammy palms, ready to experience mortifying anxiety attacks at the moment of pronouncing *pintadeau en croûte Mont-Bazillac*. New York's Le Pavillon represented the red velvet style at its absolute finest but, as with the red leatherette style, most major American cities had their versions. In Boston, it was the dining room at the Ritz-Carlton Hotel. In Chicago, Ernie "The Caliph of Caviar" Byfield's Pump Room. In San Francisco, Ernie's. In Los Angeles, the eponymous restaurant of Prince Mike Romanoff (*anciennement* Hershel Geguzin of the Riga ghetto). Crammed with antiques, top-heavy with staff, flying their red velvet like ancestral flags, these restaurants aimed—clearly with varying degrees of authenticity—to recapture the glories of the European past.

But America demanded that restaurants reflect the present. That their windows frame the Zeitgeist. No period in American history has had quite as many changes to reflect as the decades since World War II. As the United States blazed its postwar story, there was always that one restaurant whose very name seemed to capture the spirit of the times, whose address gave it a location.

In 1959, when the middle class supplanted the upper class as the major clientele, it was the Four Seasons. In 1975, when California supplanted France as the source of culinary inspiration, it was Chez Panisse. In the 1980s, as the restaurant world came to mirror the franchise nation we've come to know, it was Spago. Today, it might be said that the restaurant world has branched in two directions. While master restaurateur Sirio Maccioni is deservedly exploiting the brand-name recognition of his restaurant Le Cirque by opening in Las Vegas, another restaurateur, Danny Meyer, is attempting to fuse the scale necessary for economic survival with the idealism of much smaller restaurants in his acclaimed series of establishments around New York's Union Square.

This is the story of those restaurants, and of the people who created them and of the ways in which they have transformed the face of American dining. In many ways, it was a clash of principles. European gastronomy was about the few. The American market was about the many. When they came together, they created a whole new restaurant form: the modern American restaurant. This is the story of the men and women who made the seemingly impossible work.

The book begins in 1939 with the arrival in New York of Henri Soulé (the man whom upon his death in 1966 the *New York Times* would eulogize as "the Michelangelo, the Mozart and the Leonardo of the French restaurant in America"). He came to open the French restaurant at the World's Fair in Flushing, Queens, and went on to open the famed Le Pavillon in New York. He not only brought over the highest standards of French cuisine (making the restaurant something of a biospheric experiment on whether it could survive on American soil), but he literally embodied all the elitist notions of European gastronomy. In the story of his rise, glory, and fall are reflected many of the conflicts that have taken place in the heart of the American restaurant business—between access and restriction, between being true to one's national identity or its Americanized version, between the food that one loves to eat and that which one needs to serve.

But it is not just the story of Henri Soulé. It is also the story of some of the people who have created our modern culinary world. Of personages like Julia Child and larger-than-life personalities like James Beard. Of natural-born salesmen like the wine merchant Sam Aaron, who shook the cant out of the European wine world, and bon vivants like Lucius Beebe, who made a career from keeping it in. It is the story of men who went into the restaurant business out of economic necessity, like Sirio Maccioni, and women who went into it out of political conviction, like Alice Waters. Visionaries like Joe Baum, who are gone, and others like Danny Meyer, who is vitally active. But most of all it is the story of the American dining public. The ones who showed up through all the changes, with an eager palate, with what M.F.K. Fisher would call a "bold knife and fork." The legions who were convinced that the fine-dining experience could be transformed from just being a choice between red velvet and red leatherette. And who only needed to take their place at the table for that process to start.

CHARCOAL-BROILED

The function of the Pump Room flunky is not alone the proper service of a meal which may itself suggest the Great Fire of London destroying St. Paul's. He subtly insinuates, as well, that the only people he is accustomed to serve are from the class that throws away its Lincoln roadsters when the ashtrays are full.

—Lucius Beebe

Cafe society's four strongholds are the Stork Club, El Morocco, Twenty-one and the Colony. Twenty-one and the Colony do not even have music.

—New York Times Magazine, 1946

FIRST BITE

Just off the Avenue de l'Opéra in Paris, not far from the neighborhood known as Les Grands Boulevards, in the tiny Place Gaillon, is the Restaurant Drouant. It is painted appropriately enough the same dove-gray as a boulevardier's spats, and in the same spirit the entire building is rakishly well maintained. The first-floor windows have potted carnations, the corner molding reads "Drouant 1880," and the oyster displays are backed up against the outside walls, shielded from the passing traffic by a bank of sculpted shrubs. It is a few minutes' walk from here to the Palais Garnier opera house and only a slightly longer stroll to the Comédie Française and the colonnaded gallery of the Palais Royal. It is, however, a long way from here to a reclaimed landfill in the borough of Queens, New York, though that is where this quintessential *Belle Époque* restaurant may have left its most lasting mark. It was from Drouant and its sister restaurant, the nearby Café de

Paris, that a group of restaurant workers would embark to open the restaurant at the French Pavilion at the 1939 World's Fair. The fair was held within sight of the Manhattan skyline, on a piece of land that *Life* magazine, even as it tried to promote the fair, could only describe as "a desolate, swampy, stinking expanse called Flushing Meadow." The French Pavilion was meant to communicate something finer, a certain idea of France—and in a very Parisian way, it did. The second-floor balcony of the restaurant looked across the Lagoon of Nations with all the elegant entitlement of the terrace of Fouquet's on the Champs-Élysées, as if its every fluttering parasol were announcing to the country that the French had arrived.

The president of the fair, Grover A. Whalen, wrote that it "was built and dedicated to the people." Brotherly spirit was in the air and the theme that the entire fair was centered around was nothing less than "The World of Tomorrow." In the real world of tomorrow, Hitler would be invading Poland on September 1 of that year; but in the world of tomorrow the way the organizers meant it, everyone would have a GE toaster, a Chevy in the driveway, and AT&T long distance. Subtlest of all the promotional devices was the concept of audience interaction. The hard sell would have introduced a jarring note within the communal spirit of the fair and so, instead of simply showing a product as one did in a showroom, corporations showed Americans how the products worked. Thus, a market segment became "an audience," a sales floor became "a diorama," and a pitch "a demonstration."

At General Motors's "Futurama" exhibit, fairgoers could gaze at Norman Bel Geddes's design for a city surrounded by fourteen-lane highways that somehow managed to be both car-filled and fast-moving. Meanwhile, AT&T provided a balcony where three hundred people at a time could listen in on one lucky person's free long-distance conversation. GE brought its audience in by having engineers put five million volts of electricity through a hot dog to see if it would cook. (It wouldn't; it simply tasted burned.) Among international participants, the English may have failed to understand the subtlety of the interactive method when they brought the Magna Carta, an object that could not be bought. The French did not make that same mistake. They did not bring Gobelin tapestries or the *Mona Lisa*; they brought a restaurant that could seat four hundred, Le Pavillon de France.

The team of men who would work at this restaurant had been put together in France like specialists for a heist. The chef had been chef at the Hôtel de Paris in Monte Carlo; the sous-chef had worked at La Coupole in Montparnasse. Even a minor fish cook like Pierre Franey had been well trained in the kitchens of Drouant. The front of the house was taken care of by Monsieur Drouant himself, while the day-to-day operation was run by the maître d'hôtel of the Café de Paris, unknown as yet but soon to be mythical in the American restaurant world, Henri Soulé. Picked by Monsieur Drouant, backed by the French government, transported by the ocean liner that was the pride of the French Line, the *Normandie*, they disembarked at Pier 88 in the spring of 1939 and took their first steps in America across the still-cobblestoned Twelfth Avenue.

May 9, 1939—two days after President Roosevelt officially opened the fair—was a busy day at the Flushing fairgrounds. At the AT&T Pavilion, with three hundred people listening in, a member of the crowd, Carl Joss, Jr., put through a call to a certain Mrs. Alberts in St. Cloud Minnesota. ("Hello, is this Mrs. Alberts?" the *New York Times* reported the conversation as starting. "This is Carl. I got a lucky number at the World's Fair so I'm able to make this call free.")

"What's that?"

Carl Joss, Jr., undoubtedly used up his three free minutes explaining to Mrs. Alberts how it came to be that the American Telephone and Telegraph Company was giving away free phone time. Meanwhile, Mayor La Guardia, appearing unannounced at the Italian Pavilion, made a plea in two languages for world peace. Some of the attendees failed to understand either one of them and replied by shouting "Viva Mussolini!" and bursting into the Fascist hymn "Giovinezza."

At the French Pavilion, the restaurant opened with a gala meal. Served to Mr. and Mrs. Grover A. Whalen, the French ambassador, Count René Doynel de Saint-Quentin, other dignitaries, and 275 guests was the following menu:

Double Consommé de Viveur
Paillettes Dorées
Homard Pavillon de France
Riz Pilau
Noisettes de Prés-Salé Ambassadrice
Chapon Fin à la Gelée d'Estragon
Cœur de Laitue Princesse
Fraises Sati
Frivolités Parisiennes
Café

A meal that the *Times* translated in the next day's edition as "Chicken consommé with twisted cheese sticks, broiled lobster with cream sauce served over rice, saddle of lamb with potato balls and stuffed artichokes, cold capon with aspic, and asparagus with French dressing served on lettuce leaves, strawberries with ice cream and whipped cream, with petit fours and coffee."

As lacking as the translation is, it does communicate the exoticness with which French food was perceived at the time (and, more subtly, the fact that the dishes were unheard-of by most readers), but the article does not claim that such food was actually unavailable in New York because, in fact, it already was. Perhaps not at the wholly American restaurants like the Stork Club or the "21" Club, but certainly at a select few French-influenced restaurants. Escoffier himself had opened the kitchens of the Pierre Hotel in 1930; and at the Ritz-Carlton Hotel, the famed chef Louis Diat not only created soups like vichyssoise but also dishes named after Hollywood stars, such as Chicken Gloria Swanson. At the Colony, on Sixty-first Street near Madison Avenue, the favorite restaurant of New York society— the polished owner, Gene Cavallero (who in the circuitous genealogies of the restaurant business would employ as a young captain Sirio Maccioni, who would go on to open Le Cirque) could, with the help of his French chef, also have produced such a meal. But he probably would not have had it translated, the understanding of the time being that if you needed to have it translated, you probably couldn't afford it.

At the Colony, the ladies' bathroom was famously filled with yapping lapdogs, and the dining room a sea of tables of ladies in hats with their fur coats draped over the back of their chairs. Here, the sense of clubbiness was so pronounced that the author of the restaurant's history, Iles Brody—described by his publisher as "informal, witty and urbane"—saw fit to describe the scene when someone who did not belong dared to venture in. "When perchance an unfamiliar face appears in the doorway of the dining room, all conversation within stops, forks on their way to lovely lips pause in midair, and you, newcomer, find yourself the focus of beautiful and inquisitive eyes of patricians." Anyone with a taste for twisted cheese sticks who would be uncomfortable being the focus of all this patrician attention was out of luck.

The restaurant of the French Pavilion would change that. The day after the opening gala, the average fairgoer arrived. In the first month of operation, the restaurant served 18,401 meals. In the second month, that number increased to 26,510. This was a restaurant very much in the spirit of the fair. The experience offered was not that of some wonder of technology but of dining in a French restaurant. Here, the restaurant itself was the diorama, eating was the audience participation, and, most prophetic of all, gastronomy was the product.

Grover A. Whalen may have cared about "the people" but Henri Soulé had only ever cared about the *right* people. In this regard, the configuration of the dining room at the French Pavilion could not have pleased him. Every table spread out over the five semicircular tiers looked out across the Lagoon of Nations toward the massive statue of a heroic worker that crowned the Soviet building. It wasn't that the view bothered him, it was that every table had the same view. No table, therefore, was better than any other one, thus denying him the opportunity to show preference to a customer and to display the true artistry of the classic French maître d' that is not a dainty show of carving but rather the expertly delivered snub. This was an area of expertise in which Henri Soulé had had the very best training that France could provide.

A portly five-foot-five-inch native of a hamlet near Bayonne in the French Basque country, Soulé followed the classic waiter's career path, going through all the stops at a very high speed. First as an apprentice at the Hôtel Continental in Biarritz, continuing up in Paris as a waiter at the Hôtel Mirabeau on the Rue de la Paix; he was a twenty-three-year-old captain at Claridge's on the Champs-Élysées and eventually assistant maître d' at the *Michelin* three-star Café de Paris. This last restaurant was managed by the famed restaurateur Luis Barraya, brother-in-law of Jean Drouant, who also managed the Pavillon d'Armenonville and the Pré Catelan in the elegant Bois de Boulogne (and, yes, Fouquet's). It is a list of names that is definitive of a level of elegance that certain French restaurants excel at and for which, ironically, they use an English word to describe—they call it *le standing.*

To understand where *le standing* comes from, we must review a little bit of history, going back to the late-nineteenth century when the future King of England, Edward VII, was still Prince of Wales. The prince loved Paris. He loved the theater, the sensuality of the cocottes. He loved to get away from his long-living mother, Victoria, whose shadow stretched from Balmoral Castle in the Scottish Highlands to wherever in England he might happen to be, and, as much as anything else, he loved the food. The French language, slow to give a compliment, flung verbal bouquets at him by the adoption of certain words, all with vaguely Edwardian connotations. In Proust, the cocotte Odette de Crécy finds Charles Swann—her future husband, a member of the ultraselect Jockey Club and friend of the Prince of Wales—not "*très chic*" but "*très smart.*" There were words that related to clothing: "*le dandy,*" "*le smoking,*" "*le Prince de Galles*" (plaid). There were words to describe activities: "*le tea,*" "*le steeple chase,*" and words to describe certain types: "*le turfman*" and, more pointedly, "*le snob.*"

When in Paris, Edward enjoyed being hosted by the French Rothschilds, most notably Baron Alphonse, a practitioner of what has been called "the modified Rothschild style." (The full Rothschild style, as interpreted by Alphonse's father, James de Rothschild, may have been too difficult to reproduce, since culinarily it involved having the great Carême as your personal chef and the purchase of not only Château Lafite the wine but also Château Lafite the château.) The modified Rothschild style was thus best represented in Alphonse's Paris town house—known in French as a *hôtel particulier*—on the Rue Saint Florentin, where in an atmosphere of footmen and Louis XVI furniture, with views of both the Tuileries and the Place de la Concorde, the future King of England could dine in a setting that was suitably royal.

It didn't take long for someone to realize that the modified Rothschild style could be modified even further and that the select and private atmosphere that reigned on the Rue Saint Florentin could be kept select but made public. That person was the hotelier César Ritz.

The core belief of all Ritz properties was that if only for an instant guests should be able to feel that they were not in a hotel but in a *hôtel particulier*, a town house suitable to a member of the highest stratum of society. To achieve this, one did not just need the right food, for which Ritz had Escoffier, nor the right mix of Louis XIV antiques and a Regency setting. One needed a sweeping staircase. For that, Ritz turned to the master of the sweeping staircase of the period—the Royal Automobile Club in Piccadilly and a Warburg residence among them—Charles Mewes. The staircase that Mewes put into the Paris Ritz captured perfectly the dream that Ritz was trying to create. In a world of sweeping staircases, every bellhop was a footman, the lobby was a ballroom, and the fantasy that one just might be at Alphonse de Rothschild's was complete.

In fact, it was the Rothschilds that were at the Ritz. Among everything else that went on during the opening party of the Paris Ritz on June 5, 1898, Ritz's wife, Marie-Louise, found time to note that "the Rothschilds were there en masse." No less an authority on social nuance than the Prince of Wales understood what Ritz hotels achieved. "Where Ritz goes," he once said, "there I go."

From Ritz's point of view, it may have been too close a connection. In 1901, Queen Victoria did finally die. Edward immediately became king and his coronation ceremony was scheduled for the summer of the following year. Four days before it was to be held, the king developed a severe case of appendicitis. Ritz's Carlton Hotel in London was stuffed with royals from around the world (the procession itself was to pass right in front of the flower-laden balconies). In his memoirs, Escoffier, the chef at the Carlton, the man whose kitchens were now horribly overstaffed and whose pantries were monstrously overstocked, is tellingly reticent on the subject. "The following banquet was prepared for the gala planned to be held at the Carlton Hotel on June 24, 1902." Significantly enough, in terms of the culinary tradition of *le standing*, the same twisted cheese sticks that garnished the consommé in Flushing, Queens, were to grace the third of twelve courses of Edward VII coronation gala. Ritz did not take the appendicitis crisis quite as equanimously as Escoffier did. On the day it was announced that the coronation was postponed until August 9, he presented himself at the door of the dining room, repeated the news to the gathered dignitaries—who immediately canceled their stays—and then he went home to Golders Green and took to bed with a case of nervous exhaustion from which he never fully recovered.

Escoffier and Mewes would go on. Their particular gifts would intersect again when Edward VII's nephew, Kaiser Wilhelm II, decided to upstage the titans of British ocean travel, White Star—the company that would build the *Titanic*—and Cunard, with the ships of Germany's own Hamburg-Amerika Line. The *Amerika* was to make her maiden voyage in 1905 and the kaiser wanted it to be the most elegant liner that ever sailed. For that, he turned to the two Frenchmen. Mewes would be in charge of the staircases; Escoffier would look after the food in the small and very exclusive Ritz-Carlton Restaurant. The kaiser could only have been pleased when upon its arrival in New York Harbor, the *Amerika* was described by the *New York Herald* as "a floating St. Regis," referring to what was then considered the ultimate American interpretation of Edwardian grandeur, the hotel built by John Jacob Astor (who drowned on the *Titanic*) that opened in 1904 just east of Fifth Avenue on Fifty-fifth Street in New York.

It was directly across from the St. Regis that Henri Soulé—after working the 1939 season in Flushing, then returning to France to join a machine-gun company in the French army before being sent back to Flushing as manager of Le Pavillon de France for the 1940 season (by order of the French prime minister)—opened his New York restaurant. He shortened the name to Le Pavillon, put up Paget murals of the chestnut trees of the Champs-Élysées, and on October 15, 1941, opened for business. He invited the Vanderbilts, the Cabots, the Rockefellers, and the Kennedys for that first evening. He served them a set menu of caviar, *sole bonne femme*, *poulet braisé au champagne*, cheese, and dessert. And when it was over, he went upstairs to his changing room where he kept the tuxedos he wore for dinner and the blue suits, white shirts, and Macclesfield ties he would wear for lunch. He thought of all the people, including his wife, who because of the war could not be with him and he cried.

But let's not leave Soulé like this. Let's fast-forward several years to the glorious period of postwar New York, a city that Jan Morris, quoting John Cheever, describes as filled with "river light." It is in that light, on a bracingly cold winter's day, that we stand at 5 East Fifty-fifth Street before the restaurant's awning. Its three lines read:

5

Henri Soulé

Le Pavillon

Because it is a ground-floor restaurant, there is no possibility of a sweeping staircase for customers to make *la grande descente*. Consequently, the front door becomes the focal point of the restaurant, and just as on all great ocean liners where the best tables were always the ones closest to the staircase, at Le Pavillon, the best tables are those closest to the door. Soulé has seven tables right at the entrance. He calls it *"la Royale,"* the waiters call it "the blue-blood station." It is filled with the now mainly forgotten titans of Café Society: the Comtesse Camargo, who gave legendary parties at her estate in Cuba, Dubonnet, the Duchess of Windsor, Colonel Benes, and Cole Porter. But let's deny ourselves, for now, the experience of being the recipients of Henri Soulé's sizing-up should we venture in the front door and instead move just a few steps to the right to a more battered door from behind which the slightly insane sounds of a lunchtime service going at full speed emanate. It is the service entrance and let us instead pull this door open.

Here, there is a stairwell; the steps are dark with a compacted coat of grease left by deliverymen's work boots. We descend. The first people we see are two New York police patrolmen, in from the cold, warming themselves with big bowls of pot-au-feu that they rest on stacked cases of leeks. We pass them and, as we approach the kitchen, the noise level and sense of tension increase. Many of the menu items are cooked au gratin, under the salamanders. Because the only way to keep the salamanders hot enough to perform the gratin but not so hot that they will curdle the sauce is to intermittently throw water underneath it, the cooks are essentially working in a steam bath. These are men many of whom came over to work at the World's Fair, who are in America but not quite here. They may catch the IRT to Brooklyn every night after pulling their daily double shifts, but they still send their white bonnets back to France with friends who work on the French Line to have them pressed by nuns who, because of their own veils, are experts in pressing pleats into starched cotton.

We go up the busy stairwell that leads to the dining room, following a waiter carrying a silver serving dish with a rack of lamb surrounded by a *bouquetière* of tiny perfectly turned vegetables, and we slip inside just as the swinging door closes behind us. At the *Royale*, Cole Porter is still beaming at the recent memory of seeing the entire score of "Begin the Beguine" laid out in truffle notes on the surface of eighty eggs in aspic that were served at one of his private parties. Meanwhile, at his table, Joe Kennedy is tucking into his favorite order of veal chops Orloff, a dish that as proof that *le standing* could survive two world wars had been served by Escoffier himself to the ship-fixated kaiser aboard the *Imperator* in 1913. Soulé is happy also. The dining room is filled with the right people and everything is going well.

As the waiter puts the lamb dish down on the gueridon, or small table, from where it would be served, the customers who have ordered it look up in admiration. Soulé beams in a very French way. He is going to show them how it is done. He shoots his cuffs to better show off the cuff links that are a gift from the Duke and Duchess of Windsor (or, historically, from the grandson of the man whose appendicitis attack caused César Ritz to have a nervous breakdown) and begins to carve. Outside on Fifty-fifth Street, two strangely contented-looking patrolmen walk straight past all the double-parked limousines, both feeling the warm glow of a sensation wholly new to them—the taste of French food.

⊏=⊐

BOULEVARD
DES ITALIENS

I write about the entrance through the service door because for many years that was how I entered restaurants, as a cook. The last kitchen job I had in France, before coming to the America, was working at an all-night brasserie in Paris on the Boulevard des Italiens. They were so cheap in that restaurant that the first thing they taught me was how to apply butter to the sandwiches they sold at the counter with one movement and then to take it all off as you swept the knife back. My companion, who split the baguettes that I would then go through the formalities of buttering, called it the "Auvergnat backhand." I didn't yet know the reputation of the natives of the Auvergne region for economy and thrift and I asked him why. "The Auvergnat," he explained, "are our French Jews." I let that one slide. I was trying to pass at the time. Pass as an Auvergnat.

The Auvergne is a poor region in the Massif Central, around

the industrial town of Clermont-Ferrand, and the region's inhabitants, when they leave to find work in Paris, often end up owning a café-tabac or a brasserie. The way you get a job in one of these places is to buy their weekly newspaper, *L'Auvergnat de Paris*, in one of the handful of kiosks around the city that sells it, read the help-wanted ads, and then fake some sort of connection to the place. For the French, it is easy. They simply pick out a village name from the listing in the back, gauge its size by whatever information the town fathers have sent in to the newspaper's offices—for example, how many hunting licenses were issued that season—and invent a long-deceased grandmother who came from there. Dishwashers from Mali whose teeth are orange from the betel nuts they chew to give them energy in the draining humidity find it more difficult to fake these credentials. But they know the drill: any connection to the hard workers of the Auvergne will do and so they simply claim to have worked with someone who came from one of the region's hamlets. That is the tack that I took. With my dark, curly hair, the owner took me for a Moroccan come looking for a job. With my American passport, he didn't know what to make of me. But when I told him that I'd worked with someone from the hamlet of Meyrignac-L'Église in Corrèze, (démographie 97: 1 décès) I was in.

I'd spent four years in the kitchens of France. I'd cleaned wild ducks in the basement of the Restaurant Guy Savoy when he still had one Michelin star and we'd play rock music stations during the prep and where it was so hot in the tiny kitchen that in the break be-tween the lunch and dinner services, we'd hang our wet jackets over the ranges to dry. I'd worked at a place near Invalides called Chez Françoise, where I'd learned to make huge trays of mackerel in white wine and where the clientele was mostly politicians who would cross over from the French parliament. Here, the rosy-cheeked Breton chef had a screaming fit on the half hour, but every night, before catching the train back to his suburb, he would appear in the kitchen with his acrylic cardigan zipped all the way up to his neck, his wet hair combed across his forehead like a naughty but repentant schoolboy's, and leave us with a meek "*Bonsoir, les gars.*" I had gotten to know provincial France, down in Burgundy, at Restaurant Lameloise, just south of Beaune, near the famed wine villages of Meursault and Puligny-Montrachet. At this *Michelin* three-star, old men in blue overalls would cycle to the backdoor with baskets of sorrel they had cut on nearby riverbanks hanging from their handlebars. In summer, after the dinner service, in a bend in the road that marked the Place d'Armes, the cooks would knock back beers under the Kronenbourg parasols of the local café while the customers we'd just served would sip at their cognacs and *marcs de bourgogne* on the restaurant's terrace.

Now I was back in Paris. I was twenty-two and working the night-to-dawn shift at an all-night brasserie while living in the only place I'd been able to find, a maid's room near Place de la Bastille where the only running water was from a spigot out on the landing. I was looking for a break and that last restaurant provided it.

There was one real Auvergnat working in that kitchen: a young man named Ludovic. He'd arrived in the kitchen delighted to be working in Paris, but he was growing visibly disenchanted by the reality of what a cook's life in Paris was like. He'd been at the onion soup station for months. This meant that every day he had to peel, slice, and sauté the sacks of onions that were required to make the hundreds of portions of this soup that warmed customers all through the day and sobered them up all through the night. His frustration was only augmented by the fact that he was the only true Auvergnat in a kitchen full of people pretending to be and was forced constantly to come to the region's defense.

If anyone in the kitchen said anything particularly stupid, someone else would invariably shout out, "Tell the patron we found another Auvergnat!" with which Ludovic would mutter something about the mishmash of races he found himself among until someone convinced him that it had been meant as a joke. But his patience had its limits. Matters came to a head when one of the Malinese dishwashers somehow got two consecutive days off—an unheard-of treat. Before he left, he did a little imitation Auvergnat clog dance around the kitchen and, egged on by the laughter of the entire kitchen, said he was going down to *le pays*, or the region of France he called home.

Ludovic was slicing his onions on the meat slicer, as he always did, with a pair of motorcycle goggles underneath his toque to keep his eyes from tearing up. "We love pork down in the *pays*," he said, crossing the kitchen and grabbing a slab of pork belly from a cutting board as he went. With that, he shoved it in the dishwasher's face.

Amadou, the dishwasher, was the strictest Muslim who worked there; so strict, in fact, he wouldn't even drink beer. To have raw pork pressed into his face was enough to make him want to kill, and with that clearly in mind, he picked up a cleaver.

This is how I still see it. A group of about ten men forming a monumental sculpture (cooks in white toques, dishwashers in damp T-shirts, the Ceylonese oyster-shuckers who'd run in from outside dressed as Breton fishermen, the waiters, true Parisian *garçons*, in floor-length white aprons) all clamped around Amadou and Ludovic as we tried to keep the strong arm holding the cleaver up in the air. The funniest aspect was that as we lurched out the swinging kitchen doors and slid across the length of the dining room, we all suddenly grew silent and seemed to freeze in our positions thinking that this might just be enough for the customers not to notice us.

Tumbling onto the sidewalk of the Boulevard des Italiens brought us to our senses. Amadou needed his job, he had a large family depending on his paycheck at home. Ludovic was on his own kind of career ladder. Eventually, he would graduate from onion soup, master a limited repertoire of brasserie dishes, and one day, possibly, even be considered for a position as sous-chef. We may not have been Auvergnats but we were French enough to realize that management would not feel that order had been reestablished until dossiérs, or reports on what had happened, were filled out.

As soon as we got back into the kitchen someone handed out the blank forms and we started to write, leaning on the clean parts of counters and helping each other with the grammatical points. It was fairly amusing that the only person who knew the kind of French that, if they were to sound official, the reports required was Amadou. "You have to use the *subjonctif*," he offered.

"What's the *subjonctif*?" Ludovic asked sheepishly.

"*Il a fallu que je fasse*," said Amadou giving an example.

"Ah, that's the *subjonctif*."

We had gotten the correct tense straightened out when Madame, the wife of the patron, stormed into the kitchen. She was furious. "Happy now?" she barked. "You all get to run back in here. Did you notice you knocked the Paris-Brest off the dessert cart? I had to stand out there with *crème pâtissière* all over my shoes."

What was commendable about the French, I thought, was that at no point in the ensuing conversation would the impressions of the customers on the scene they'd just witnessed come up. Epithets had been used, cleavers had been raised, *crème pâtissière* had been spilled, but no one cared about the customers.

"We're filling out the paperwork, Madame," I offered, pointing out that we were following correct procedure and were now well past the cleaver stage of the evening and into the *subjonctif* stage.

"Too perfect," said Madame, glaring at me. "Now I have a *bougnoule* telling me he is filling out the right forms."

Bougnoule is one of the most insulting terms in French, used as an epithet for anyone dark-skinned or of Muslim or African extraction. Anyone who, clearly unlike Madame, could not trace their line all the way back to Clovis, king of the Franks.

"I am not a *bougnoule*, Madame," I said calmly, as if replying to her insult were just a point of order, "I am an American."

This statement, sounding so confident in its identity to others, resounded in my inner ear because of its falsehood. I had probably spent, over several visits, no more than three months in the United States, each time going simply to visit my grandparents, who lived in New York. But no one else knew that. My father had left in 1952, to write poetry in Europe—a picture showed him in a camel hair coat on the deck of a ship leaving from Hoboken. In Spain, he'd met my mother, a traveling Irish girl from County Cork. After their divorce, I'd gone with my sister and mother to live in Ireland, where I'd spent from age eight to eighteen (or what the Irish call "the deformative years"). A year at Trinity College in Dublin spent reading Descartes's ontological argument proving the existence of God had sent me running to Paris to learn something slightly more concrete: cooking. With an entire kitchen looking at me, it was now clearly over. I took off my apron, balled it up loosely, and left it on the counter. "*Au revoir*, Madame," I said and I walked out past her.

I walked that night, feeling at loose ends from the half-worked service, with my knives tipped with wine corks from the restaurant so they wouldn't cut through the paper bag in which I carried them. I joined in with the crowds strolling along the Grands Boulevards in the summer night. They were taking in Paris, but I was saying good-bye. I knew that my next job would not involve the help-wanted pages of *L'Auvergnat de Paris* but rather the use of my American passport. The realization came to me on the steps of the Palais Garnier, looking all the way down the Avenue de l'Opéra. Drouant was only three blocks away and I didn't even know it.

⬅➡

"LUSCIOUS LUCIUS"

Along the first-floor balcony of the "21" Club in New York, the cast-iron jockey hitching posts, painted the colors of the great American racing stables, stand stoically facing out at all the changes that have taken place on Fifty-second street. Below them is the famous grill-work gate through which all the customers pass through. Just to the right is the service entrance. It was through that door and down the steep steps that lead to the basement that I entered my first kitchen job in the United States. The scene at the bottom of the stairs was action-packed. The stock boys would be filling the cold rooms with produce, while their boss, chief steward Charlie Matola, in his white shop coat, baseball cap, and thick glasses, would invariably be waving a sheaf of receipts in the face of an impassive deliveryman. Farther down the corridor was the silver-burnishing room, where a steward spent the day feeding cutlery into the rotating drums filled with ball bearings. At the end of the corridor were the butchers, standing over huge wooden blocks and cutting down into prime Black Angus beef. I would grab a uniform from the open cages in which they were kept and change out of my street clothes in the locker room. Then, with my knives under my arm, I would do a sort of stutter-step between traffic as I went down the corridor toward the first-floor kitchen. On my right, between stacked tables, was the secret entrance to the cellar that during Prohibition the Feds had never been able to find.

There was one cardinal rule for my station: Make sure that the cream sauce for the chicken hash was as thick as paste. If it wasn't, several bad things happened: the diced chicken breast would not get properly coated, the sauce would seep through the sherry-scented wild rice that surrounded the dish, and, worst of all, when put under the salamander before being sent out, the dish would not gratinée properly but would burn.

Because chicken hash was one of the restaurant's signature dishes, before the service, the restaurant term for the duration of a meal, just about everyone in a position of importance checked on the consistency of the sauce. The chef, Alain Sailhac, tasted it. The legendary gentlemen of the restaurant, Jerry Berns and Pete Kriendler ("Mr. Jerry" and "Mr. Pete"), would occasionally peer in on the cooking line from between the metal bars of the pass-through and offer a concerned smile. Then came some of the men responsible for the table assignment once the service started, famed maître d' Walter Weiss and manager Ken Aretsky. These were men confronted daily with the darker aspects of the human ego—"21" may have cast-iron jockeys and grillwork, plenty of history, rooms full of Remington cowboy sculptures and style, but everyone knows that though there are 120 tables in the joint, only 40 of them count.

In the kitchen, the services were brutal. One five-hour-long blur of nicely gratinéed chicken hash orders, beef rib eyes cooked well done, double servings of beluga for the Wall Street baby moguls,

Walter Cronkite's VIP order, and off-the-menu orders for chipped beef, an ungodly mix of rehydrated meat, béchamel, and hollandaise, which reminded the billionaire veterans of their days in the service.

To come down from these huge services we would drink. First at Hurley's on Sixth Avenue next to Radio City, then often continuing in the after-hour clubs in Spanish Harlem where the Dominican dishwashers would take us. There was salsa in the jukebox, Löwenbräus on the counter, and cocaine in the bathroom. The illegality of it all was part of the fun, and I always got a kick out of knocking on these unmarked doors around 126th Street, where a little wicket would open to check us out because a little wicket opening to check out customers is exactly how the venerable "21" Club had once operated seventy-four blocks to the south and about six decades earlier.

Restaurants have the ability to frame the historically momentous within the confines of their windows. Haute cuisine, for example, came out of the French Revolution. When Beauvilliers opened one of the very first Paris restaurants, La Grande Taverne de Londres, in 1782, he promoted himself as an "*ancien officier de Monsieur le Comte de Provence*" or ex-officer of the Count of Provence. It was a portentous distinction. By 1793, the count's older brother, Louis XVI, had been led to the guillotine and the aristocracy's cooks had been sent looking for jobs. (Not that they quickly forgot their ex-employers. In a perverse French twist, the word *Thermidor* is both the name of a particularly bloody period of the Republican calendar—Thermidor 9 Year II, or July 27, 1794, being the day that Robespierre, as per Carlyle's description, went to the guillotine wearing "sky-blue nankeen trousers"—*and* a nineteenth-century mustard-tinged recipe for lobster au gratin.)

Not quite as epic as the French Revolution but momentous nonetheless, many of the great New York restaurants of the 1930s and 1940s came out of a different kind of social upheaval: Prohibition. At

"21", they had collapsible shelves, while at the Colony, Gene Cavallero kept his booze in an elevator so it would never be on the same floor as the raiding Feds. Frank Costello bankrolled Sherman Billingsley's Stork Club and it was rumored, though never established, that the silent partner behind Henri Soulé was one-time bootlegger Joseph Kennedy. If the great names of French cuisine—Carême, Dubois, Escoffier—could have come out of a culinary pantheon, the names that were central to the post-Prohibition restaurant world—Mr. B., Mr. Pete, Jack and Charlie, Mr. Gene, and Mr. Joe—could have come out of a Damon Runyon short story.

Yes, there were restaurants before Prohibition. Broadway was packed with lobster palaces. Eighth Avenue around Midtown was filled with the sort of restaurants that A. J. Liebling described as having "vaguely French table d'hôte dinners and Italian proprietors." "In those basements," he continued, "middle-class New Yorkers were taught that the ultimate in desserts was a pancake that burned with a wan flame." Meanwhile, at Luchow's, the great German restaurant on Fourteenth Street, one could not only eat Wiener schnitzel in a genuine beer hall atmosphere, but also buy goose fat by the quart to take home. As popular as these and many others were, the two restaurants that defined turn of-the-century dining in New York were Sherry's and Delmonico's.

Over the years, since the Delmonico brothers opened their first café in lower Manhattan in 1827, the famed restaurant had several locations. At each one, they encapsulated the ultimate in big city dining. Morse telegraphed the first cablegram to London from the dining room of Delmonico's (receiving his reply in forty minutes, to the wild applause of 150 guests). Tammany Hall's Boss Tweed delighted the invited pols when he created an artificial lake in the same dining room and filled it with swans for the reception following his daughter's wedding.

Sherry's, meanwhile—by 1898 it was facing Delmonico's

across Fifth Avenue at Forty-fourth Street—was a restaurant that police officers with names like "Whiskers" Chapman might raid for holding stag parties at which the guests were being entertained by less than fully clothed dancers with names like "Little Egypt." It was also the restaurant of choice for the coming-out parties of the daughters of the German-Jewish banking set. If the management of the restaurant was unclear as to which exact market segment they were going after, the customers were not. In the 1927 novel *Red Damask*, by Emanie Sachs (as in Goldman, Sachs), a character voices the opinion that "there isn't a house we don't go to, including Sherry's, that hasn't a damask wall." The important word here is "house." To a certain extent, these restaurants were private. If they weren't restricted to a family, they were certainly restricted to a class.

But a new class came up with Prohibition, one that was conflicted between its wish to be seen in select company and, at the same time, to see as wide a dissemination of this news as possible. The newsman's flashbulb might pop in the dining room, but the velvet rope at the door made sure that most people didn't get any closer to the scene than the next day's newspaper. By the time the Eighteenth Amendment was repealed in 1933, this nighttime living, publicity-generating crowd was being referred to as "Café Society." Just inside the door of El Morocco sat the perfect decoder of café society's schizophrenic message, Lucius Beebe. A square-jawed Boston Brahmin with features not unlike Jimmy Cagney's, a taste for fine suits, and a column called "This New York," which ran from Topeka, Kansas, to Anchorage, Alaska, on the *New York Herald Tribune* syndicate.

Christened "Luscious Lucius" by his only real competitor, Walter Winchell (table fifty of the Cub Room of the Stork Club), Beebe was wholly lacking in Winchell's sinister attachment to power, though he compensated for it by his obsession with class. Expelled from both Yale and Harvard ("I'm sorry to send you such a bad potato," Yale's President Angell wrote Harvard's President Lowell), the twenty-seven-year-old Beebe was given his column in 1929 because it was thought that he would be among equals. Soon, however, he was better known than most of the people he was supposed to be covering. By 1937, he was the subject of a two-part profile in *The New Yorker* entitled "The Diamond Gardenia," in which the writer described Beebe's beat as dealing "almost exclusively with perhaps five hundred patrons in four or five restaurants." In 1939, he was on the cover of *Life* with the caption "Lucius Beebe Sets a Style." Photographed wearing a gray top hat, a checkered waistcoat, and a watch chain made from mother lode gold, he embodied in his person a very real sense of class distinction while fully appreciating the promotional value of the restriction itself. When it came to those "four or five restaurants," the hook for the reader was that they couldn't get in.

Beebe had his own inimitable style. Children where simply described as "rancid issue," his objection to a new-model Rolls-Royce was that it was unfortunately "suitable to be driven by its owner rather than a lackey." Money was his favorite subject; it invariably came in "blizzards of currency" or was represented by "a flood tide of imperial sables." For full effect, the Beebe style required both a commitment not to leave any alliterative possibility unexplored and a belief that the conventions of product placement must always be satisfied. San Francisco on a junket thus smelled of "money and Mornay," while the martinis served at the Colony—where in a secret deal with owner Gene Cavallero he ate at a 60 percent discount—were indeed "as clear as one of the Van Cleef and Arpels diamonds in the lobby display."

Though dismissed by some as no more than "a sandwich man for the rich," Beebe would never be vulgar enough to love money per se; instead he loved the drama of promotions and sales. He had begun writing his column in the year of the Wall Street crash, when the good life was little more than a front maintained by everyone in the hospitality business. If the famed Theodore Titze of the Ritz let him live for free in the hotel, it was so that others might be encouraged to spend at the sight of this well-tailored person "bountifully stoked with foie gras and forty-year-old Hennessy." When a newly opened restaurant was suddenly filled with beautiful young couples ordering magnums, Beebe delighted in knowing that it was simply because the services of a casting agency had been retained. The restaurant world that he loved didn't just include French chefs and Italian maître d's but a netherworld of publicity agents and managers, casting agents and impeccably dressed shills. In essence, it was the total opposite of the civilized fantasy that the restaurants were trying to create.

In the April 1946 edition of *Gourmet*, in the "Along the Boulevards" column he was writing at the time, Beebe gave his list of the ten best restaurants in New York City. In alphabetical order they were: Baroque, Chambord, Chateaubriand, Colony, Jack and Charlie's ("21"), Lafayette, Luchow's, Le Pavillon, Plaza, and Stork Club. Le Pavillon he described as "flourishing in a midst of mink and monocles, gilt and mirrors reminiscent of the best Paris restaurants." What he failed to clarify was that it wasn't the customers who wore the monocles but Henri Rouget, an old-time captain who'd been with Soulé since the Pavillon de France in Flushing. The great practitioner of the monocle was Olivier, the famed maître d' at the Paris Ritz who, with a single stare, as Beebe wrote on another occasion, "reduced demanding patrons and troublesome old duchesses to the estate of peasants." Within the American context, the monocle was more of a prop than a tool, a flourish meant to persuade the customer that the setting in which they found themselves was not a restaurant at all but something akin to a French Rothschild's mansion. It was *le standing* by way of Midtown New York.

This was the goal in all of the most French-influenced restaurants that made up Beebe's list, and they had several ways of achieving it. In a magnificent misuse of space—in an inch-conscious business— couples at these restaurants sat along banquettes facing outward toward the room rather than in the more constricted tête-à-tête. Jewels helped, and to this end, the best restaurants had paying arrangements with the finest New York jewelers to keep a selection of diamonds in display cases (usually near the bar) that might induce the rich patrons to visit the stores (Cartier always at Le Pavillon). A dress code was important, too. Though dinner clothes were not actually required, neither were they discouraged. Soulé himself never relaxed the dress code enough to welcome a man to dinner wearing a shirt any other color than white. The fantasy was best achieved by the delicacy with which the customer was handled. First of all, as in any decent mansion, there was some room-to-room movement. One could order while seated at the bar, and when the meal was ready, the maître d' in his most Proustian manner would address himself to the hostess and say, *"Madame est servie."* Since kitchens prided themselves on being able to satisfy every whim, one could order off the menu and no experienced chef would dream of going into a service without a supply of peeled white grapes for the inevitable orders for sole Véronique. One was served in the most elegant style of all, which is not the "French" or "English"—which respectively means serving oneself and being served from a platter on one's left—but "Russian," a style that was brought to France by the Russian ambassador in 1810 and that means the captain serves from a gueridon. The table, it almost goes without saying, belonged to one for the evening. Even in an American version of a French fantasy of a Rothschild's palace, one didn't "turn" the tables.

What really nailed the fantasy was that at the end of the meal, one didn't pay. Since credit cards were not yet invented, restaurants offered their own version of credit—the house account. The Colony had thirty-five hundred, and at one stage, Le Pavillon had eight thousand. While carrying so many accounts turned the restaurateur into a banker—and often a debt collector—in Soulé's mind, it was a worthwhile trade. Extending or denying credit gave him the power to decide just who got into his restaurants, and that level of control, after all the effort he put into it, was exactly how he wanted it to be. *"Le restaurant,"* he was given to say, *"c'est moi."*

But what about the food at these restaurants? At the Stork Club, the scene was the reason to go and the kitchen could get away with dishes such as lamb chops Saint Hilaire, which, as grand as it sounded, was, in fact, an unappetizing lamb chop stuffed with chicken hash. The menu at Le Pavillon, where the food was among the many reasons to go, did not try to impress with any unnecessarily grand-sounding names or fin de siècle ostentation. There were no fish mousse constructions, no presentation more elaborate than *langouste en Bellevue*. The cooking style was delicate in terms of simplicity and skill, as in *potage Germiny* and *billi-bi*, respectively the consommé and mussel broth soups that require last minute "liaison," thickening with egg yolks and cream.

Simply put, these were some of the most pedigreed dishes of the French repertoire served within an American context. The context could, at times, be unintentionally funny, as with the veal chops Orloff that Joe Kennedy so liked to eat. Making veal chops Orloff on Fifty-fifth Street (a dish invented by Urbain Dubois, who apprenticed at the Rothschilds', who employed Carême, who worked for Talleyrand, who nationalized Church property prior to the French Revolution) may have been only six degrees of separation from the beheading of Louis XVI. But serving it to a man who had made his fortune in the machine-gun-fought Scotch wars of Prohibition was seven.

"THE AMBASSADOR IN THE SANCTUARY"

But there was another kind of food served at Le Pavillon. One that Henri Soulé did not promote. Every day, he had the chef prepare fifteen or so portions of a *plat bourgeois*, dishes such as pot-au-feu, choucroute, or cassoulet, which he kept off the menu and which he alone could suggest to customers who he sensed would appreciate them. It was the sort of food that he himself liked to eat. One of the central ironies of haute cuisine is that restaurant people often do not care to eat what they serve. The food is too rich, too distilled, and perversely unappetizing when dealt with every day. At no time is this more evident than when a French chef visits a colleague in his kitchen. He may sneak a look at the latest creations flying out the kitchen door on tray after tray, but the hosting chef will know better than to actually offer his colleague any of these dishes to eat. Instead, he'll cut down the saucisson that he's been keeping for just such a special occasion (the drying saucisson hanging by a string from a pipe in the wine cellar, in all likelihood), and together they'll stand by a cutting board in the kitchen happily slicing and eating saucisson while the service continues around them.

For all his airs, Soulé was no different. In New York, he may have been an increasingly famous personage, but on return trips to his native Basque country, he strolled around in a houndstooth cap and a light wool sweater buttoned all the way up to the bottom one of his many chins, every round inch the proper provincial *monsieur*. While in Paris during the 1950s, he didn't eat at any of the *Michelin* three-stars of the period—Lapérouse, La Tour d'Argent, or even the lodestar of Le Pavillon, Le Café de Paris—but at Le Grand Comptoir, the bustling brasserie near the heart of Les Halles where at lunch the tables were filled with prosperous produce agents and the long zinc bar was three-deep with vegetable porters peeling hard-boiled eggs and knocking back the green-stemmed shots of white wine known as *petits blancs*.

Two magazine profiles of Soulé published in 1953 captured his contradictory sides. The first one, entitled "The Perfect Restaurateur," was published in *Holiday* and was written by Lucius Beebe. The style is typical. The carpet at Le Pavillon he declared to be "deep enough to be negotiated with snow-shoes," while the long-stemmed roses that decorated the tables seemed, to Beebe, to "reek of well-being." The most memorable aspect of the article—certainly in hindsight—is the full-page black-and-white photograph of Soulé about to serve caviar. He is wearing a perfectly fitting, clearly custom-made, double-breasted tuxedo. His shirt and pocket handkerchief are starched stiff. He hovers delightedly over a gueridon on which are placed all the necessary ingredients of proper caviar service. Nestled in a silver bowl filled with crushed ice is a four-and-a-half-pound tin of beluga, beside it some toast points in a starched linen napkin and little dishes filled with finely chopped parsley and separately chopped hard-boiled egg whites and yolks. In Soulé's manicured hands are three soupspoons. He is about to serve the reader. Behind him, out of focus, the unmistakable mustachioed visage of Salvador Dalí, who dines with a lady in one of the banquettes. Staged as it is, this is the face that Soulé presented to the world. This is veal chop Orloff Soulé.

The second profile published in 1953 shows the other side of Soulé. Entitled "The Ambassador in the Sanctuary," it was written by Joseph Wechsberg and appeared first as a profile in the *New Yorker* and eventually became the book *Dining at the Pavillon*. The article has myriad scenes. There's the Soulé who "pilots" guests to their tables, the Soulé who enjoys seeing French boxer Marcel Cerdan fight, Soulé at his weekend house in Montauk feting a birthday with a handful of friends. They drink, they cry, they stop for hot dogs at a roadside hut on the way back into Manhattan. For all the good cheer, the overall image that comes through the article is that Soulé, despite his success, feels alienated to a surprising degree from his adopted country.

"I left Saubrigues twenty-five years ago," he confides to Wechsberg at one stage, "but I'm really still there." As if to prove it, he proceeds to give the recipe for what to a Basque is always the symbol of home, *Maman's brandade de morue*: "Maman would cut the cod into small pieces and poach them for about ten minutes. Then, after removing the skin and bones, she'd mix in slices of potatoes she had boiled in their skins, and add oil, garlic and chopped parsley. She always served the brandade de morue neither hot nor cold but just tepid. What a dish, what a dish! Sometimes when I went home for a holiday I'd eat it morning, noon and night."

It is startling to hear Soulé speak in such a heartfelt manner. It was a point of professional pride with him precisely not to open up. Aimé Thélin, his cellar master for over twenty years, was the only person in New York allowed to call him Henri. Meeting customers of Le Pavillon on liners on return trips to France, he would never sit with them for fear that it would lead to familiarity—on their part—when they met again at the restaurant. He may have opened up to Wechsberg because he sensed in him a different shade of his own sense of cultural displacement.

Joseph Wechsberg (it amused him to go by "Joe," the Americanized version of his name) was the genuinely sophisticated version of Lucius Beebe. If Beebe's idea of shilling was to eat at the Colony at a huge discount, Wechsberg's main experience with the art form was as the one-time head claqueur of the Vienna Opera House where, as a well-dressed plant in the audience, it was his job to drive the applause through all of its encores.

Fleeing Europe after Hitler's occupation of his native Czechoslovakia, he fought in the U.S. Army and after the war joined in the exodus to Hollywood, where he quickly failed at screenwriting. He turned to fiction, allowing his blurbs to describe him as "knowing the shoddy chic world of smooth opportunists and gullible Americans." But it all came out sounding like bad Beebe: upwardly mobile and slightly inconsequential. In *The Continental Touch*, a character spotted on the Promenade des Anglais in Nice "had the elegantly subdued tan known as the Riviera tan, a lighter more expensive shade of the Arlberg or St. Moritz tan." This from a man who could describe Vienna as "a city in G-minor" because that musical key best expressed "Vienna's ever present mixture of gaiety and sadness, euphoria and gloom, cheerfulness and resignation." Wechsberg, a Moravian, would always feel closer to *Mitteleuropa* than to mid-America. For him, the melting pot was not Manhattan but his beloved Vienna, with its Hungarians, Slovenes, Croats, and Bohemians; the river of dreams was not the Hudson but the Danube. It would be this ability to communicate many of the essential subtleties at the heart of the European character that would eventually make him such a widely read, and much admired, magazine writer. With no subject did he go into greater nuance than in his writing on food.

Thus, in *"Tafelspitz* for the Hofrat," an essay on Viennese boiled beef collected in his 1948 classic *Blue Trout and Black Truffles*, he wrote, "In Vienna there was a restaurant that was held in high-esteem by local epicures for its boiled beef—twenty-four different varieties to be exact. The restaurant was called Meissl & Schadn, an eating-place of international reputation, and the boiled beef specialties of the house were called *Tafelspitz, Tafeldeckel, Rieddeckel, Beinfleisch, Rippenfleisch*. . . . The terminology was bound to stump anybody who had not spent the first half of his adult life within the city limits of Vienna. It was concise and ambiguous at the same time; even Viennese patriarchs did not always agree exactly where the *Weisses Scherzl* ended and the *Ortschwanzl* began." The passage is typical Wechsberg: informative and bemused, its jaunty tone tempered by such a plangent use of the past tense as to communicate that not only has all the boiled beef been eaten, but the world in which it was eaten has been destroyed.

In the 1953 profile of Soulé, Wechsberg brought all his European subtlety to bear on the inescapable comparison between Soulé and the greatest restaurateur in France, Fernand Point. Six foot three and weighing over three hundred pounds, Point seemed to encompass in his wide girth many of the schisms at the heart of French cooking: between Paris and the provinces, between food that is refined and food that is hearty, between dishes named after thin-blooded French aristocrats and dishes such as choucroute, cassoulet, and bouillabaisse. From 1925 until his death in 1955, Point manned the stoves at his legendary restaurant La Pyramide, in the town of Vienne, just south of Lyons and in that period managed to change the entire focus of French cooking.

Point's version of regionalism was magnificently inclusive. His menus included the blue-legged chickens of Bresse, the crayfish of Lake Annecy in the Alps, the hams of the Morvan, the prime beef of the Charolais, and the freshly landed fish of the Mediterranean ports. Though he'd trained in the haute cuisine style at the Hôtel Bristol in Paris, he preferred to change his menu daily than to crank out the classics. He didn't really want a restaurant but a country inn. According to Wechsberg, when people first opened their napkins at Point's, they could smell the sunny fresh air and grass on which they'd dried.

It was just the sort of touch that made him legendary. In 1930, he married Mado, the local hairdresser (usually characterized as being "indomitable"), and by 1933 he had been awarded his third *Michelin* star. Later he would have in his kitchens a band of raw apprentices named Bocuse, Troisgros, and Chapel, who would carry on his legacy. Customers often started out their meal with Point's famed crayfish gratin and ended it with the hazelnut-scented marjolaine cake that Point is credited with inventing. In between, over several courses, was a meal that signaled an entire sea change in which restaurants went from being all about status to all about food.

If achieving this in the heart of provincial France was hard, matching it on East Fifty-fifth Street was all but impossible. "I'm convinced that Soulé has done well by the French cuisine," Wechsberg quotes Point as saying, "but after all how French can any French restaurant be in America?" Despite Soulé's best efforts, there were several conceptual differences. First was the question of how much time was devoted to a meal. At La Pyramide, lunch was a virtual photo op of the ideal France; a long affair that Wechsberg had described as being eaten "at the round table under the plane trees of the garden terrace." In New York, on the other hand, Soulé told Wechsberg, "If I were to insist that my customers take their time, I would be out of business tomorrow." Second was the matter of seating. While the customers who made the pilgrimage to La Pyramide—knowing they closed the door when the dining room was full—were simply grateful to be sat, in New York their happiness all depended on *where* they were sat. The key section of real estate at Le Pavillon was the tiny space by the front door where the customers could study the comings and goings. This was "the sanctuary" of the article's title. "Today, space in the sanctuary is at such a premium," Wechsberg wrote, "that some people appear delighted to eat at tiny extra tables hastily set up in the middle of the aisles there during rush hours, or so close to the revolving door that they are constantly fanned by it. 'They would rather dine in the telephone booth than in the *salle*,' Soulé says, with only a momentary lifting of the eyebrows."

But the main difference between the two men was the type of food that each was able to serve. Point could, if the mood so took him, put a dish such as choucroute with purée de pommes on a menu that also included a sophisticated dish such as *brioche de foie gras*. Soulé, on the other hand, simply could not. The choucroute, by its very name, defined brasserie cooking, the French antithesis of the atmosphere he strove to create and a style that veal chop Orloff Soulé definitely could not promote. Why? Because not every customer was a Wechsberg who understood French subtlety. They thought that the compliment was when Soulé himself spooned out your caviar, not realizing that the real compliment was when he whispered in your ear about the bistro classic, *tête de veau vinaigrette*. Here, surely, was a situation that would make anyone misty-eyed for *Maman*'s *brandade de morue*. Despite all his success and the profiles in the national magazines, Soulé could not print on his own menu the sort of food that he himself liked to eat. It would have overly complicated things. In America, you stayed on message. Every bistro owner in a beret knew it, every Spanish waiter stamping out a flamenco number as he presented the paella knew it, just as it was known in every Chinese restaurant where fortune cookies were constantly handed out and by every Italian waiter belting out "O Sole Mio" as he strolled between his tables. Soulé, too, had to stay on message. Wearing a blue suit at lunch, a dinner jacket at dinner, standing, glaring, snubbing, spooning, and constantly carving. Other restaurateurs were prisoners of a national identity imposed on them with their arrival in this country, he was a prisoner of *le standing*.

FLAMBÉED

We wrote a letter to Whirl, telling them we would do the booklet, providing we could segregate the recipes and not be credited with those which we feel are done better with butter—that we like Whirl for certain things. I cannot see myself selling it. It looks like something for artificial insemination when it comes out of the can, and I'm sure it is going to have that effect on most who see it.

—James Beard, letter dated June 22, 1956

I'll be doing a series of cooking shows on WGBH-Channel 2, Boston starting in January. Every Thursday evening from 7.30 to 8, beginning Jan. 3rd. If the station reaches into your territory, I'd like to know how you think the shows are. They're going to have a bit of fancy knifework on most every program.

—Julia Child, letter dated December 16, 1962

"LIVE NOW, PAY LATER"

In March 1956, when my grandfather retired as the head of the advertising department of Ludwig Baumann, the furniture store that once dominated the New York furniture world, the company gave him a going-away luncheon at the Gotham Hotel at Fifth Avenue and Fifty-fifth Street. In pictures taken for the leather-bound "testimonial book," my grandparents sit at a central table wearing wan smiles. Around them at larger tables sit friends and colleagues, laughing and gesticulating over the classic components of the 1950s send-off lunch: the lunchtime tumbler of Scotch, the shrimp cocktail served on ice, the half-eaten Parker House roll. The walls of the banquet room have been quickly decorated with KLM and TWA posters showing the Eiffel Tower and the Spanish Steps in Rome, allusions to the first European trip that my grandparents would soon be leaving on.

The entire meal was, in fact, a setup. Things were not going well at Ludwig Baumann. My grandfather's send-off—something he had not wanted; a shy man, he would have preferred to slip away into his new career as a painter—was a means of reassuring guests such as the president of Simmons Mattress and the publishers of several of the city's dailies that all was well. (They bought mattresses from one and many full-page ads from the other.)

What had happened was that Ludwig Baumann was no longer the only big store to offer furniture on the installment plan. Macy's had come out with a system of paying for it on credit. It came down to image. Macy's represented quality, while Ludwig Baumann—to use the Yiddish for a retailer of poor-quality furniture—was a *borax* operation. Many years later, my grandfather explained it succinctly by saying, "A guy would rather have a Macy's truck pull up in front of his house than an LB truck." By the mid-1960s, such a simple preference would cause a store with branches in every borough and a giant flagship store on Eighth Avenue to close.

While the pictures from my grandfather's send-off lunch might be said to capture a crossroads in the world of furniture retail, they also offer evidence of two important factors that were about to transform the American restaurant business. On the one hand, air travel (as represented by the hastily put-up posters) would make Europe a real place for an increasing number of Americans, the Spanish Steps in Rome not just a drawing on a TWA poster but steps that one had actually climbed. On the other hand, the increased availability of credit would bring the gastronomic experience within reach for a social class of Americans for whom it had never been available before: the middle class. The very class that Soulé was determined to save haute cuisine from.

Soulé never really mastered English. In moments of stress, he always reverted to French. During strikes, for example, "my boys" quickly became "those *types*." One English word he was particularly proud to have mastered was "four-flushers." "I have to protect my val ued patrons against four-flushers who would like occasionally to make a big flash or consummate a business deal," he said in 1953 to an imaginably beaming Lucius Beebe. If the quote is accurate—and not polished by Beebe—it would seem that Soulé had gone to the trouble of finding a word that described, with a certain disdain, people of un-substantiated pretensions. In one telling sentence, he'd denied him-self the custom of nothing less than the two fastest-growing segments of the gastronomic dining population. First, people who may not have been independently wealthy but who were interested in food and wine and might on occasion treat themselves to an expensive restau-rant. Second, a population of business people for whom eating with clients was an increasingly important part of closing a deal. Both would soon be armed with a tool that would allow them to bypass the Soulés of the world—who would use the excuse of vetting them for credit for house accounts to vet them socially: the credit card.

In the travel section of the *New York Times* of Sunday, January 6, 1952, hidden in the pages devoted to Florida resorts, was a brief no-tice titled "On the Cuff," which informed readers that "anyone who can sign his name and pay his bills can charge his way through some of the better hotels, restaurants and night clubs of the country under a new credit card system known as Diners Club." The notice went on to explain: "So far some thirty hotels, 400 restaurants and night clubs, 200 automobile rental agencies, five florists and several other services are available to members who get one itemized statement at the end of each month. The club's office is in the Empire State Building." Of all this information, the most important is the last sentence. If you were going to slap a piece of paperboard in front of someone and hope to have it accepted as payment, it had better show a good address.

The word "credit" in the 1950s had somewhat the same power that "broadband" has today. Everyone knew it was the future but no one knew quite how it would work. The Federal Reserve fretted about what this surge in paying with credit might do to the economy. But the American public quickly set about giving the word a semantic makeover in which the concept of paying with borrowed money went from being something to be hidden to something that was displayed proudly. There were synergies: Sheraton Hotels bought 12 percent of Diners Club, Hilton Hotels started the competing Carte Blanche. There were launchings: the R. H. Macy card for the homebody, the KLM card for the traveler, the *Esquire* card for the man-about-town, and for the budding gastronome, the Gourmet Guest Club. In keeping with the shaky new principles of credit, the grand-sounding address of the magazine's editorial offices—"Penthouse. Hotel Plaza. New York. N.Y."—was printed right over the holder's name and undoubtedly more humble home address.

Launched in 1958, the Gourmet Guest Club card came attached to a wallet-sized booklet that explained how presentation of the card would entitle the holder to "credit courtesies" at all the restaurants that were listed inside. Leafing through the directory, the member of the Gourmet Guest Club could see with some satisfaction that the card was accepted from Pablo's Cuisine au Vin in Provincetown, Massachusetts, to Hellriegel's Inn in Painesville, Ohio. The problem was that when people carried around a card that read "Penthouse. Hotel Plaza. New York. N.Y.," they were looking for more than "credit courtesies" at Hellriegel's Inn in Painesville, Ohio. They were looking for that address to somehow rub off on them, to make some sort of connection between themselves and big money. They were looking for access to restaurants where without the card they may not have even dared enter. This, the Gourmet Guest Club was not wholly successful in providing.

For example, under the listing of Boston restaurants in the directory, there was no mention of the Ritz-Carlton dining room or Locke-Ober. In Chicago, a certain McNaught's New Orleans Shrimp House is mentioned but not the famed Pump Room. In San Francisco, they could have "Roast Cornish hen à l'orange garnie" at Ernie's, but there was no mention of the slightly more clubby Jack's or the Blue Fox. In Los Angeles, similarly, while they could eat with Paramount writers at Lucey's on Melrose Avenue, they could not eat with Paramount stars at Perino's on Wilshire Boulevard.

As for New York itself, where within a small radius of the Plaza Hotel could a member of the Gourmet Guest Club actually eat? At the venerable Café Chambord under the Third Avenue El they could indeed indulge in "Le homard des gourmets flambé à l'absinthe." They could even go to the Colony for "Crème de tortue" or "Faisandeau en Cocotte Souvaroff." That, however, would be the high point of their New York visit. Presenting the card would not have gotten them far at "21", as for doing so at Le Pavillon, well; one shudders at what might have been the reaction.

Soulé did not believe in credit, he believed in house accounts. When he offered customers a house account, he was guaranteeing them that when they ate at his restaurant, they would find themselves among their own class. It was an exchange of favors. If they paid on time, he allowed them, the ultimate in urbanity, to simply get up from the table at the end of the meal and leave him to initial the check and fill in the tips for the waiter, captain, and sommelier. Having a house account was proof that you belonged.

Not having a house account got you a different treatment. There was always the possibility of paying with cash, a form of payment that allowed the restaurateur the opportunity to perform the traditional ritual of skimming the till. But it was not encouraged; the more people paid in cash, the greater were the chances that the coveted "good" clientele would not find themselves among their own. Paying by check was not encouraged either. If you wrote your own check, it was simply not accepted. Instead, you were presented with a blank house check that you not only had to sign but also back up with several pieces of identification. While the waiter went back and forth with the reams of paperwork that this transaction produced, you were clearly communicating to the surrounding tables that you were not part of the regular crowd.

If you had the temerity to actually request a house account, you had better already have a strong sense of self-worth. Soulé was once interrupted with a request for a house account just as he was about to perform some tableside carving. He undoubtedly bestowed a wreathed smile on the man before pointing him toward a door just off the dining room where he told him to wait. Each time the man reappeared from the bathroom, Soulé pointed him back inside. The puzzled man finally understood the message and left. For Soulé, house accounts had a philosophical implication: they were not means of getting people in, they were a way of keeping them out.

Diners Club, however, would not be kept out and persisted in their efforts to have their card accepted in good restaurants. In 1959, they organized a "progressive dinner party" for journalists where each course was served in a different New York restaurant that accepted the card. The meal began with shrimp and crabmeat wrapped in crepes at the Colony, progressed to the Sheraton East for "Borscht and Piroshki," and on to Café Chauveron, where Roger Chauveron served "Poulet Sauté au Vermout." By this time, enough Haut-Brion '53 had been consumed for the Diners Club executives to start singing the praises of living on credit to the assembled representatives of *Look*, *Cue*, the *Journal-American*, the *New Yorker*, and Craig Claiborne, the food editor of the *New York Times*. "Someday there won't be any money; there's really no need for cash," Mr. Matty Simmons, a Diners Club VP, was subsequently quoted as saying in "The Talk of the Town." "No money, and there'll be no robbery, no holdups, no worry about losing one's money."

A group of people who knew a thing or two about the worry of losing one's money had been watching developments from their fortress at 65 Broadway in downtown New York. For American Express, the reason they had not gotten into the business of credit was the fear that it would destroy their highly profitable traveler's check business. But in a country where Pan American Airlines encouraged people to travel with the "Fly now, pay later" pitch. Where upon arrival at the destination Diners Club took the relay with their "Live now, pay later" campaign. (An approach to travel, in essence, in which a vacation could be enjoyed without the use of a single traveler's check.) Within this environment even American Express understood that it had to go into action.

They came in like Bigfoot. They did not want to be one more credit card company; they wanted to be the only one. After toying with the idea of buying Diners Club outright, they instead bought the 40,000-strong membership of the Gourmet Guest Club and the 120,000 card-carrying members of the American Hotel Association, and they were in the credit business. Not satisfied to promote their card with clubby "rotating dinner parties" like Diners Club, in 1963, three years after its launch, American Express loaned $300,000 to a restaurant management firm to complete what was then one of America's first stabs at a food court. The complex included the Trattoria, Charlie Brown's, a "Victorian City Pub," and Zum-Zum, a rapid-service Bavarian-sausage counter restaurant, all on the main concourse of the Pan Am Building on Park Avenue.

It was indicative of the lengths that American Express would go to in those early days of credit that in order to have their card accepted by a restaurant, they would help to build the restaurant. There was only one restaurant management company that would have understood such a convoluted approach, and that was exactly whom they loaned the money to—in exchange for having the card accepted not just in the Pan Am Building but also at their many restaurants. The company's name was Restaurant Associates and in the tradition of the restaurant business they were known as RA.

BEARD AND BAUM

As far as the Flushing fairgrounds may have been from the Avenue de l'Opéra, a good case could be made that from the swamps of Newark, New Jersey, to the heights of New York, restaurant sophistication is even farther. That, however, is the journey that RA made in the 1950s. The year 1953 may have been the *annus mirabilis* of coverage for Henri Soulé, with his profiles by both Beebe and Wechsberg, but it was also the year in which RA opened its first real restaurant, the Newarker, in Newark Airport. They were given the location because by the reasoning of the Port Authority of New York and New Jersey, any outfit that could turn a record profit at the airport concession stands by selling oversize twelve-inch hot dogs for 15 cents should be able to turn the trick again in a restaurant with tablecloths. And by force of planting sparklers in the desserts, serving three-clawed lobsters, and a barrage of publicity, they eventually did. On the day they "served one thousand customers," or "one thousand covers," the restaurant name for an amount of customers served, the staff celebrated. The chef took ball bearings from the silver-burnishing machine and threw them along the kitchen floor to terrorize the waiters. The manager broke open the champagne. Later that night, after much more champagne had been consumed, the beams of a car moved slowly through the fog that envelops the inlets of the Newark marshes. It could have been a mob body drop-off except for the incongruous sounds of a Swiss oom-pa-pa tune being hummed by the man walking slowly in front of the car trying to keep the driver from veering off the road. This was the Newarker's chef, Albert Stockli, a man who unbeknownst to himself would become one of the most influential chefs working in the United States. Behind the wheel, the restaurant's thirty-four-year-old manager—small, dapper, usually intense but right now laughing, Joe Baum, a man who by the end of the decade would supplant Henri Soulé as the driving force of the New York restaurant world.

The concept of taking money from American Express was not at all alien to RA. It was the same idea from which they themselves had evolved. In their earliest incarnation as Wechsler and Sons, Coffee Importers and Roasters, they sometimes helped finance the chains of coffee shops that would use their coffee exclusively. In a 1964 profile of the company in the *New Yorker*, Abraham Wechsler described the process: "Our first real participation in the business was in the nineteen-thirties, when we came to the rescue of the old Silver's Cafeteria chain, one of our largest customers, which had overexpanded in the depression. . . . I converted their debt to us to an equity position—half of their company. In 1942 Riker's Restaurant Associates, a chain of thirty-five small coffee shops, also ran into trouble—among other things most of their countermen had been drafted—and the next year I arranged for Silver's to buy its stock."

By 1945, the company's name had been shortened to Restaurant Associates and after a succession of vice presidents had died on the job, Wechsler put his twenty-five-year-old son-in-law, Jerry Brody, in charge of running it. Brody, an Air Force veteran and a graduate of the Amos Tuck School of Business at Dartmouth, quickly set about trying to improve the quality of the restaurants. While he instituted blue-plate specials such as "Chicken with Burgundy Wine," his more important contribution was the institutionalization of what would be RA's cardinal business rule: always let someone else pay as much of the rent as possible. A typical arrangement was the one he had with Ohrbach's department store. Ohrbach's owned the employee cafeteria, RA ran it. In a similar way, by 1953, the Port Authority had offered them the Newarker. Despite initial misgivings as to the location and their own ability to run a real restaurant ("None of our places in those days had waiters," Abraham Wechsler told the *New Yorker*), Brody was ready to seize the opportunity. To facilitate the transition from countertop to tablecloth, he hired Joe Baum.

A graduate of the Cornell University School of Hotel Administration and an assistant to the industrial designer Norman Bel Geddes (who designed the Futurama exhibit at the 1939 World's Fair), Baum was working at a Schine Hotel in Boca Raton, Florida, when he was contacted by Brody. He was an RA natural: he worked long hours, could crunch the numbers, and, as Wechsler said approvingly, "didn't traffic in kickbacks." With the eventual success of the Newarker—it took two years; the first year they lost $25,000—he was quickly made a vice president of the company. Then things quickly started to change. Baum's idea of who would get the honor of helping to pay RA's rent was of a different order of magnitude from Ohrbach's department store and eventually read like a who's who of corporate America. The list of the buildings where RA had restaurants included Rockefeller Center, the Time-Life Building, the Pan Am Building, and the Seagram Building. As impressive as the list reads, the leases with these landlords were not reached by any carefully thought out business plan but with RA's inimitable blend of serendipity and hustle.

If they got their first restaurant by proving they could make a profit on hot dog stands, the way they got their second one was no more complicated. In the innocent spirit of the times, someone mistook an award the Newarker had received from a cutlery industry group for an award from a gastronomic society and took a risk on them running the Hawaiian Room in the Hotel Lexington. A quick trip to Hawaii was enough for Brody, Baum, and Stockli to acquaint themselves with the culinary traditions of the islands, and back in New York they set about promoting their new restaurant. Arthur Godfrey, the television host, happened to stay at the hotel and in a spirit akin to a Marx Brothers routine, the three principals of RA replaced the room service meal he'd requested with a meal that—early fusion—displayed the traditions of the Hawaiian table as envisioned by the Swiss-born Stockli. ("I knew Godfrey was a ukulele player," Brody allowed to me many years later by way of explaining the germ of this particular idea.) Godfrey liked the food. Within a few months, *The Arthur Godfrey Show* was being broadcast live from the Hawaiian Room.

They were moving at a speed that was capturing the attention of some of New York's most important landlords. One night, after dinner at the Hawaiian Room, the president of Rockefeller Center, Gustav S. Eyssell, told Brody that he had a Forty-eighth Street location that he just might be interested in. Brody didn't take long to decide. As *Fortune* put it, "People like Restaurant Associates just don't say 'no' to the Rockefellers."

So they had a new landlord with deep pockets. Now they had to find a theme for the restaurant. Because all the capitalist might assembled around the location put the RA brain trust in mind of imperial Rome (and because their designer had recently purchased twelve large moldings of twelve Roman Caesars), they soon had it. The Forum of the Twelve Caesars on the ground floor of the U.S. Rubber Building would be the best imperial Roman restaurant in two thousand years. To learn the necessary traditions, they were off again, this time to

Rome—where Brody and Baum picked up a taste for black Brioni suits—Pompeii, and Herculaneum. Back home, they didn't let up. The chefs were given Apicius to read while the wait staff's reading matter was Robert Graves's translation of Suetonius's *The Twelve Caesars*. In the interest of absolute authenticity, the entire staff was treated to screenings of Mervyn LeRoy's *Quo Vadis* (with Robert Taylor and Deborah Kerr).

Today, the culinary glory of imperial Rome is no longer reflected in the vicinity of Rockefeller Center. The Forum has been closed for many years. No more sparklers are lit in Newark Airport. No more hulas danced at the Hawaiian Room. The only restaurant from RA's heyday that is still open is the one that was its greatest achievement: the Four Seasons in the Seagram Building in New York.

When the blueprint for the building left architect Mies van der Rohe's desk, it did not include plans for a restaurant on the ground floor. But as the building slowly went up between Fifty-second and Fifty-third Streets across Park Avenue from the equally modern Lever House Building, Jerry Brody saw that it would make a great RA location. It was going to be the most talked-about building in New York and the landlord had plenty of money. A first move in the campaign to get it was to invite Phyllis Lambert, the daughter of Seagram head Samuel Bronfman, out to lunch. An art patron who lived in Paris, she was determined to make the Seagram headquarters a triumph of modern architecture. With that in mind, Brody (in a limousine rented for the occasion to make him look like someone who could talk about corporate headquarters on Park Avenue) drove her out to the Newarker, the one restaurant that could pass for modern in the RA stable. The idea that he tried to impress on her over lunch was synergy: whatever the Seagram company ended up putting on the ground floor of their new building should reflect the product they sold. Since liquor was their product, food was a natural match.

A whole six months went by before Brody was summoned to

"Mr. Sam's" office in the Chrysler Building. "I hear you want to open a restaurant," he said, pausing to allow Brody to go into "a polished oration" whose flow was in no way impeded by the fact that Mr. Sam was soon asleep. The rapid tapping of a pencil against the desk by his son woke Mr. Sam up in time for the oration's stirring conclusion: a world-class building could only benefit from having a world-class restaurant on the ground floor. With an "All right, my man will meet with you," Mr. Sam gave it to them. "They wanted us," Brody would recall. "They thought we were experts."

RA now had the location. The problem with the synergy argument now became apparent. The building was indeed daringly modern, with famously controversial nonloadbearing, "decorative" girders. But what was a daringly modern restaurant? The RA brain trust knew that here they couldn't just stick sparklers into the food as at the Newarker. This wasn't Newark; this was Park Avenue. They couldn't just hope that some moldings their designer had stored in a warehouse would give them a design idea. This building would be the epicenter of the "less is more" school of architecture and the restaurant would eventually have thirty-foot-high bare wooden walls. Scariest of all, they couldn't even be French.

Joe Baum was too self-aware for that. "It wouldn't have been too difficult," he admitted to *Holiday* magazine soon after the restaurant opened, "to induce some celebrated Parisian chef to come over for a fabulous salary and allow him to pick his own staff of countrymen and compose his own menus. But, after all, we are not Frenchmen, we are Americans. How could we hope to compete with a man like Soulé, who is not only a Frenchman to his toe-tips, and a genius in the bargain? His restaurant is really French. Ours would be an expensive counterfeit."

Counterfeit is an interesting choice of words for the vice president of a company with the corporate approach to authenticity that RA had. But it is indicative of what they intended the Four Sea-

sons to be. It would be their great restaurant. Yes, there would be liv-
eried doormen and live trout tanks reminiscent of some of the great
restaurants of France, but there would be no hiding behind antiques
or sauces named after long-dead French nobles. This was epochal: an
attempt to shear the presence of France from the very idea of elegant
dining. A separation of form and function, substance and style, tradition and historical context. At the Four Seasons, the "modified Rothschild style" would meet the Mies van der Rohe style and someone
had to come up with a menu. Had the RA brain trust gone a restaurant
too far? No translation of the classics would help them here. Nor
would sending the staff to any screening. It was RA's good fortune
that along the road of success from Newark, Joe Baum had picked up
the services of the larger-than-life, tweed-clad, Falstaffian food consultant James Beard.

James Beard was at the forefront—when not actually the cre-
ator—of most food trends in this country for four decades. Whether it
was making hors d'oeuvres in the 1940s, writing about Parisian restaurants in the 1950s, about outdoor cooking in the 1960s, or the pleasures of homemade bread in the 1970s, he was always there with a
book and his theatrical persona performing demonstrations for the
American public. It was at times a financially perilous existence.
Though his cocktail party catering company, Hors d'Oeuvre, Inc.,
proved to be a reasonable success (it got a write-up from Lucius
Beebe), personal differences with his partners caused it to close. By
1950, he'd come and gone from *Gourmet* and by 1954 he'd been hired
as a consultant by Joe Baum.

"I am starting to work as a consultant on a full-time basis for
an organization known as Restaurant Associates," he wrote to his California friend and fellow cookbook author Helen Evans Brown. "The
first thing is to develop rum drinks, then inexpensive dishes with
wine and so on. They are a wonderful group of people and I am only

hoping to know what they want as clearly as they seem to know it. I shall take you to their top place at Newark Airport when you are here." But it was also one job among many. In his youth, Beard had trained for a career in both opera and acting and after he turned his attention to making his living in food, he put those theatrical gifts to good use. Department store demonstrations alone could have kept him working on a full-time basis. His letters voice their tiresome toll. "I did another Bloomingdale's stint this morning. . . . In Dallas, at Neiman's I have to do flaming foods one afternoon, cold foods for a buffet another, and then one afternoon on tablesettings, glassware and how to use it, and all that sort of crap." There was something small-scale about such demonstrations that grated on Beard, particularly when compared with the sheer piston-driven dynamism that RA soon took on.

What Beard saw in RA was that within the confines of the theme restaurant world, they were as genuine as could possibly be. This was a country where "Trader Vic" Bergeron allowed customers to stick an ice pick into the wooden leg he claimed to have lost to a shark when, in fact, it had been lost to a bout of childhood tuberculosis. Where a serious magazine such as *Holiday* could judge Chicago's Pump Room to be the very definition of class because this was a place "where waiters waltzed in bearing flaming food on swords, where Nubian coffee boys strutted around in headdresses crowned with three-foot-high ostrich plumes and Martinis were served in stemmed soup plates." Within this context, watching *Quo Vadis* was a serious stab at authenticity, and authenticity would always be the most important component of any Beard recipe.

Good food for Beard was food that had "a homely quality"—the phrase with which he praised the cooking style of his one-time student Marion Cunningham. He was able to find it in the gestures of a short-order cook near his Greenwich Village home who, to Beard's delight, "would make hash-browns by pressing cooked potatoes down on the griddle with an empty coffee can." He was able to find a more sophisticated version of this authenticity in a 1955 list he drew up of his favorite restaurants in the United States. The quality was present in the simmered dishes of Le Pavillon just as it was in a order of shad roe with crispy bacon served on the red-checkered tablecloths at "21". He could find it in the oysters Rockefeller served on a bed of rock salt at Brennan's in New Orleans and in a sherry-scented portion of lobster Savannah at Locke-Ober in Boston. It was definitely apparent in the grillroom atmosphere of Jack's on the slopes of Nob Hill in San Francisco and in the leather-lined booths of Musso and Frank on Hollywood Boulevard. The menu of the London Chop House in Detroit, with its broiled whitefish from Lake Superior, perch from Lake Ontario, and—read it and weep—baby frog's legs from Lake Michigan seemed to encapsulate it. Rounding out the list are the restaurants Quo Vadis in New York and Perino's in Los Angeles, two restaurants that, though owned by Italians, didn't offer too much more of their native cooking style than an appetizer of *pastina al uovo* to be followed by the chef's interpretation of some classic from the continental cuisine repertoire. It is curious that there is not one truly Italian restaurant on Beard's list, particularly since Italian food, for us, has come to define homeliness itself.

"My opinion of Italian cookery is not too high," he wrote from France in 1955. "And getting my first piece of French bread on the train yesterday made me realize again what masters the French are at the art. It seems to me that even the food on the wagon-lit restaurant was better than all the food of Italy. . . . A late supper at the Régence of marrow on toast, a grilled kidney and some cheese tasted like ambrosia." The statement may be a clearer reflection of the quality of Italian food he had been able to find on his recently completed trip than on the state of Italian *cucina*, but it does illuminate the conflict that lay at the center of Beard's understanding of food. That conflict did not pit the French style against the Italian, but the genuine against the fake. The grilled kidney at the Régence obviously satisfied that criterion while a captain clicking his heels and calling him *signore* clearly did not.

Telling, in this regard, is Beard's very different relationship to two of RA's restaurants, Mama Leone's and La Fonda del Sol. RA bought Leone's from Gene Leone in 1959, the same year they opened the Four Seasons. It was not only a proven moneymaker but defined a certain culinary style. Known for its "traveling antipasto," which was carted around the dining room (which could seat thirteen hundred), Mama Leone's was the mother ship of the "more is more" school of Italo-American cooking, where quantity often won out over quality. Located in Manhattan's theater district, it originally opened only at night, but if you stuck your face into the kitchen at noon, you could see the cooks already stacking the deep-fried slices of eggplant for that night's *parmigiana*. It may have been thought of as an authentic experience, but it was the one RA restaurant that James Beard would not go near.

La Fonda del Sol, which opened in 1960, was RA's "good" version of an ethnic restaurant. At first look, it may have appeared to be a typical RA brain wave: a Central American restaurant on the ground floor of the Time-Life Building. It certainly got the RA treatment. The doorman on Sixth Avenue wore a sombrero and poncho, while the uniforms were designed by the theatrical king of thongs, Rudi Gernreich. The press was worked over ("My Sweet Sixteen Party at La Fonda del Sol," in *Seventeen*), and the restaurant's manager, in a nice RA flourish, saw fit, in the interest of authenticity, to change the name on his business cards from Frederick Rufe to Federico Rufe. But where it counted, in the kitchen, RA had the great, blind Los Angeles cook Elena Zelayeta making the *mantequilla de pobre*, the turkey in green mole sauce, the *rosca borracha*, and the tortillas. "Mix the tortillas with love," Zelayeta would say, "or they will be bitter." Beard admired her authenticity while Albert Stockli, surely delighted that he hadn't been called on to give his Swiss version of Central American food, put himself completely at her service. Where Mama Leone's was living off the memory of having a woman in the kitchen, La Fonda del Sol actually had one.

Having a woman in the kitchen had always been a clear demarcation of styles in both French and Italian food. In France, legendary restaurants such as La Mère Blanc in Vonnas or La Mère Brazier in Lyons represented a kind of antirestaurant tradition, one that was less concerned with displays of culinary virtuosity than with a faithful reproduction of their region's cooking. In Italy, where a false regionalism of dishes called *alla romana* or *alla milanese* was widespread, the role women cooks played in guarding a true sense of regionalism was even more pronounced. Italian regionalism is a factor of the country's geography, regional purity being maintained, at least in part, by such obstacles as the Apennine range, the Valley of the Po, and the Gulf of Genoa. But as Waverley Root noted in his classic *Food of Italy*, it can be broken down into smaller components than regions or even provinces. "All Italy is mountainous," he wrote, "and mountains tend everywhere to shut each valley into its own tightly closed box, with which local customs develop and harden, uncorrupted by influx from similarly cloistered adjoining valleys." These were the pocket-sized culinary regions that the women of Italy watched over. They worked in the trattorias and osterias that could be found up and down the narrow streets of any Italian town. They bargained at dawn. Met fishing boats on Neapolitan wharves, sized up vegetables for *ribollita* (twice-cooked soup) in Florentine mists, and, in Roman markets, chose between fillets of salt cod for the *filetti di baccalà* they served fried in batter. What they would have cooked at home for six or eight they then proceeded to cook for forty. And when a dish ran out, the customer didn't hear it whispered by a maître d' but from a voice that boomed from the kitchen.

Eventually, it would be this simple style that would triumph in this country, the one of the wood-fired cannellini beans, the bread soup, the pig's trotter, *zampone*. While American food and Italian food were obviously different, they did share, at their best, a certain simplicity of approach. (The equivalent gesture to a short-order cook pressing on hash browns with a coffee can might be said to be a large-armed woman in a Roman trattoria spooning pasta cooking water into a sauce to get it to the perfect consistency.) James Beard was the perfect person to bridge the differences and lay the groundwork that would eventually allow the simple Italian style to become popular, not because he understood Italy particularly well but because he had a deep understanding of America.

Beard's understanding of the ideal America was intertwined with his Oregon childhood. Frozen in perfect memory were such culinary Tom Sawyerish moments as "trekking up the Necarium River fishing for crayfish with ear of corn baits." By giving a personal resonance to ingredients—for him, the list would always include salmon cheeks and succotash—he allowed us to later appreciate their Italian equivalents from polenta to squid. The technical knowledge of simple Italian food and a love of Italian regionalism, from Tuscany to Liguria, would eventually come from writers such as Marcella Hazan, but the groundwork for that sensibility to flourish in this country was prepared by a man whose happiest moments were spent not in Tuscany but a short train ride from Portland, Oregon, "digging for razor clams in the mouth of the Columbia River."

The titles of his books—*Cook It Outdoors*, *The Fireside Cookbook*, *Jim Beard's Barbecue Cooking*, *Beard on Bread*, *James Beard's American Cookery*, to name a few—clearly communicate this internalized appreciation of food. Recipes like red flannel hash, which was "made the day after a New England boiled dinner which always includes beets," or "Harriet Coe's mustard ring with coleslaw" (Beard was not one to assume that the American experience didn't also include suburbia) communicate an emotive coefficient to these most American of foods that paradoxically would be completely understandable to an Italian.

To illustrate this parallel simplicity—this "homeliness"—in terms of ingredients, one need look no further than the almost totemic weight that American hams held for Beard. This man who could churn out words for corporate sponsors became quite lyrical on the subject. He knew the pedigree of a Smithfield: "A lean type of hog part razorback." He delighted in ham's regional and artisanal qualities: "The South has peach-fed, peanut-fed, even artichoke-fed (Jerusalem artichokes that is) hams which are cured in brine, smoked, treated and aged about three months. Throughout New England, the Middle West and the Northwest you will find good country hams." And receiving a good one as a gift was worthy of mention in a letter. "Had a small ham from the Amana Colony in Iowa," he wrote to Helen Evans Brown. "They sent me ham, bacon, cervelat, smoked sausage etc. . . . real good honest smoking, and the bacon cut from the rind, and the rind sent along for cooking." The ham may have come from Iowa, but the principle that you keep the rind of a good ham to flavor your soups and beans would have been fully appreciated by *contadini* anywhere in Italy.

The equivalent fundamental ingredient in Italian food is garlic. This bulb has always been a particular obsession of the dining public. Escoffier, a native of Provence, went so far as to not leave diners' garlic paranoia out of his memoirs. "What sir?" he recalled a horrified lady saying to him one evening after he'd given her a recipe she'd requested. "Do you mean to say you have made me eat garlic for the last three months? That's abominable! I hate garlic. I would never have expected to see it served in a first class restaurant such as this one."

More sophisticated palates than that lady's were in agreement on this point. Wechsberg's article on the famed Provençal restaurant

L'Oustaù de Baumanière was entitled "Provence without Garlic," while Samuel Chamberlain's book *Italian Bouquet*, published by *Gourmet* in 1958, reassuringly informed the reader that it was "a bouquet that does not draw heavily on garlic as is too often assumed." Into this atmosphere came James Beard with his recipe for chicken with forty cloves of garlic. Were forty cloves actually necessary? Probably not, but it was more than a recipe, it was a challenge, a confrontation with pretensions and, since the burp, the fart, and garlic breath were the actual genteel objections to garlic, a vote for pleasure over status. In the land of garlic powder, it was a testament to authenticity.

Today, "authenticity," "food memory," and "genuine" are some of the words that best describe the modern food sensibility. The words come together in Beard, who often used them, and the relationship between them is not as simple as it might at first appear. The term "food memory," for example, almost by definition includes the word "genuine" and often also "rustic." Very few people's food memory involves pheasant à la Souvaroff. By 1958, as Beard, the RA management team, and other food consultants such as Mimi Sheraton worked to come up with a menu for the Four Seasons, it became clear that by following these principles, they were moving away from the tenets of haute cuisine. The problem wasn't going to be coming up with dishes that reflected this culinary vision. The problem was that RA wanted it to be their great restaurant, and for Craig Claiborne, the *New York Times* critic who would be giving them their most important review, "very great" meant "very French."

It could not exactly have alleviated anyone's anxieties when on April 13, 1959, four months before the Four Seasons was to open, Claiborne wrote nothing less than a front-page article entitled "Elegance of Cuisine Is on Wane in U.S." The very first sentence read, "The time-honored symbols of the good life—great cuisine in the French tradition and elegant table service—are passing from the American scene." Beard earned his RA paycheck by coming through for them in the second paragraph. (The two men were, in fact, friends and would often share Christmas and Thanksgiving meals together.) Described as "a writer on cookery," Beard was quoted as saying, "This nation is more interested in preserving the whooping crane and the buffalo than in perpetuating classic cookery and improving standards of table service. We live in an age that may someday—with all justification—be referred to as the time of the decline and pall of the American palate." The quote has all the felicitous ease of the prepared sound bite, but for RA its most important clause may have been that Beard chose to say "classic cookery" and not "French cuisine." When dealing with public perceptions of what could be considered elegant dining, every word counted.

As an example of the sort of food and service he was talking about, Claiborne, it almost goes without saying, called up Soulé, who invited him to come over. Downstairs at Le Pavillon, Claiborne first met Pierre Franey, the chef with whom he would eventually team up to write the column "The 60-Minute Gourmet." Photographs of Franey making a whole striped bass stuffed with sole mousse were eventually used to illustrate the article. One can imagine the photo shoot. Franey busily beating the mousse over ice. Soulé and Claiborne both beaming, Soulé with pride, Claiborne with appreciation. This was how it was supposed to be done.

Growing up in Sunflower, Mississippi, seems not to have left Claiborne with the same appreciation for indigenous American foods as growing up in Oregon did to Beard. He had not only attended a Swiss hotel school, but his culinary epiphany had not happened at the mouth of any river but returning from Europe, on a voyage between Cherbourg and Manhattan aboard the *Île de France*. "On the first night out," he recalled in his autobiography, "what was placed before me was a dish of such stunning magnificence I felt—without hyperbole—

what amounted to a spiritual revelation. The dish was listed on the menu as Turbotin à l'infante . . . never again has anything tasted so audaciously good as that young turbot with white wine sauce."

A review of the Parisian restaurant Lasserre on the Avenue Franklin D. Roosevelt shows how much he'd internalized the great French tradition's values. "It is even more surprising that a restaurant of Lasserre's genre—grand luxe, elegant—would list snails bour-guignonne on the menu. While snails with their garlic scent are emi-nently delicious and perfectly suited to the restaurants near Les Halles or in small bistros anywhere, they are no more appropriate to a first-class restaurant than sauerkraut with beer, Limburger cheese and country wine. In such a setting the all-pervasive odor of garlic, like that of cigar smoke, becomes offensive."

This is truly French. A stratification of what kind of food is appropriate to be served in different classification of restaurants and the conviction that such "genres" should never be mixed. It is so widely instilled in the French mind that one need only open certain novels to find it voiced. One thinks of Proust's fond description of his childhood housekeeper's efforts to describe for her employers the lo-cation of a restaurant of which she approved. "It was one of those cafes where Françoise 'Thought they did know a little about cook-ing,'" Proust wrote. "But it wasn't Henry's on the Place Gaillon be-cause that wasn't 'a little restaurant.' Nor was it Webers, because she meant 'a good restaurant' and Webers was 'a drinking shop.' Ciros. Definitely not as that was a restaurant where the cooking was done 'by ladies of the world.' No, it was a place where—the ultimate com-pliment—'they looked as if they kept a very good little family table' . . . The restaurant of which she spoke with this blend of pride and good-humored tolerance was, it turned out, the Café Anglais."

To be fair, RA did understand the difference in genres as well as Claiborne. In the back of the Seagram Building on Fifty-third

Street, they planned to open the Brasserie, precisely the sort of more casual restaurant where, in true brasserie fashion, one could enjoy a choucroute. But as the Four Seasons neared completion, the RA brass, particularly Brody, worried that this would not be enough of a bow in the direction of France to please Claiborne, and as a preemptive strike, Brody invited him to come over and see what they were trying to do at the Four Seasons for himself.

His report of the visit appeared on July 16, 1959, a month before the restaurant was slated to open. In the single page devoted to "food fashions family furnishings," the headline read "$4.5 Million Restaurant to Open Here." Amidst the fact that it was nearing completion and that it was said to be the world's costliest restaurant were mentions of "the futuristic look" of the furniture, talk of the Rothkos and Pollacks that were planned for the walls, and an allusion to the financial arrangement in which Seagram was "underwriting part of the cost." Also mentioned was James Beard (this time described as "a well known wine and food authority"), who was "instructing the waiters on the history, characteristics and character of wine, as well as the etiquette of pouring it." But when it came to the food that would be served Claiborne could not forget some of the wilder fantasies that had gotten RA to this stage: the sparklers, the pineapple concoctions, all those portions of "Filet Mignon Caesar Augustus with Rising Crown of Pâté and Triumphal Laurel Wreath." In a backhanded compliment that could have done nothing to reassure Baum and Brody, Claiborne described Stockli as a chef "whose imagination is largely unfettered by European tradition."

That lack of tradition would, in fact, be what would make the Four Seasons menu great. There would be no piped "doots" (the word is Beard's) arriving before the meal from the kitchen, but freshly cut crudités; there would be "rustic" dishes such as iced periwinkles and smoked rack of lamb with minted white beans. There would be playful adaptations of classic dishes: the parfait here was herbed lobster, the vichyssoise made with apples, the soufflé with quince. Dishes such as Amish ham steak with prune knoedel had the sort of evocative name that could have just about anyone believing it was part of their "taste memory." The rolling hors d'oeuvre cart, with its wooden kegs filled with herring in wine, anchovies in vinegar, and smoked sprats, a turning wheel hanging heavy with saucissons and Italian and Smith-field hams, was a virtual monument to authenticity.

The menu set, the waiters trained, the Picassos hung, the RA brass prepared to open. Tempers were running short. A food consultant who pressed to have a wild morel garnish printed on the expensively produced menus was told by Baum, ever the realist, "If I print morels on this menu, you'd better come up with them, if you have to grow them in your armpits!" A greater cause for anxiety than the supply of wild mushrooms was the review. They'd placed their bets. They'd made the most expensive restaurant in the country and it wasn't French. What would Claiborne think?

On Friday, October 2, 1959, placed between an announcement that Cholly Knickerbocker would be reporting on the season's debutantes in that Sunday's *Journal-American* and the news that Bergdorf Goodman's lingerie department was now offering "a nylon tricot nightgown that is trimmed with dainty satin bows," the review of the Four Seasons appeared. The turned, "sculpted" vegetables in Claiborne's opinion may have needed some work, but the fact that there was no dish even resembling a whole striped bass with sole mousse and champagne sauce did not seem to present an obstacle to greatness. "It is expensive and it is opulent," wrote Claiborne in the second paragraph, "and it is perhaps the most exciting restaurant to open in New York within the last two decades." Everyone knew—and surely Soulé did if he deigned to read the review—that the restaurant that opened within the last two decades that Claiborne was referring to was Le Pavillon. Brody's hunch about the location had been right.

The originality of the building had caused American gastronomy to take one of its most significant leaps. For RA, it had been quite a journey to make. In less than ten years, they'd gone from the lunch counter, the most indigenous of American restaurant forms, to the Four Seasons, the most original of American restaurants.

⊢———⟶

"WE ARE AMERICANS"

A fully formed story seems ready to burst out of the creation of the Four Seasons. It is the story of how the face of the people creating and using American restaurants was changing. Something igneous in society sometimes surfaces in its clearest form in the bustle of a busy restaurant. Such was the case at the Four Seasons, which managed to reflect in its thirty-foot-high beaded curtains and its inner pool some of the societal changes of the late 1950s and early 1960s. Not only was the food not strictly French, nor the design dependent on antiques to impart a cultivated atmosphere, but it was started by a group of people for whom it would have been ridiculous to continue the pretense that a great restaurant was somehow connected to the aristocratic European town house. As such, it brought into focus two diametrically opposed views of the restaurant business between the American and the French.

Joe Baum and Henri Soulé embody these two divergent views. Their management approaches were different: Soulé wanted to bestow tables, Baum wanted to "turn" them. (A turn being the amount of times in a service that new customers occupy a table.) Soulé was "The Ambassador in the Sanctuary," Baum and his lieutenants in the black suits and white shirts were the restaurant version of the Rat Pack. The greatest difference was conceptual: Soulé thought of Le Pavillon as an extension of his personality; Baum called the RA restaurants "stores." Other than his unannounced, and much feared, inspection tours, he preferred to spend his time back at the corporate headquarters—in a neighborhood of body shops near Tenth Avenue—poring over blueprints for the next one.

It was a physical distance from the actual point of sale, coupled with Baum's own ruminative nature, that allowed him to see some of the more abstract facets of the restaurant business. "A problem of the business is the leftover frontier Calvinism relating to whether service is an honest trade to be in," he told the New Yorker in 1964. "It doesn't have an inner status. That's the real crux in our world. . . . If your product is food and service, you must love food and service. It isn't always easy. Our business is rife with social conflict, economic conflict, and war between the waiter and the kitchen, the waiter and the customer, and the waiter and the customer and the kitchen. Holy mackerel! Am I getting this straight?"

The narrative that encompasses the individual story of Joe Baum, the Four Seasons, and RA is one that reflects many of these conflicts. Not only was the face of the American diner changing—especially since the credit card made the restaurateur's opinion of one's social worth increasingly immaterial—but so was the face of the people involved in providing the gastronomic experience. Suddenly, the people running the most talked-about restaurants were not French, those selling wine did not have phony accents, and those writing cookbooks did not try to fake their expertise with a lot of purple prose. The food world had come to represent a much broader band of the American social spectrum than it had ever done before.

At one side of that spectrum were men, often Jews, who thought of food and wine unapologetically as a product—men like Baum or his colleague and friend in the wine business Sam Aaron or the one-time airline caterer André Surmain, who opened Lutèce in 1961. On the other side of the social spectrum was Julia Child, a daughter of Pasadena wealth who joined the OSS and married Paul Child, an official at the Department of State. When she turned her attention to French food, she brought all the refinement of her background to bear in championing and later communicating to an eager American public the genius of authentically prepared French food. Like two fronts, the Baumian and the Childian approaches converged on gastronomy in America.

Soulé was not beyond being affected by the social changes. Practically proving that the successful restaurant cannot exist in a time warp, the late 1950s and early 1960s would be a disaster for him. Credit cards he could dismiss with the same disdain that the majority of his clientele did, but the social forces went deeper than that. On the business front, he would be faced with strikes by the restaurant unions, there would be walkouts by his kitchen staff, and competing restaurants like La Caravelle, which opened in 1960, and La Grenouille, which opened in 1962, would be started by one-time employees. The social front was even more disastrous. The election of President Kennedy—a man who felt so at home in Le Pavillon that he was known for hopping down the steps into the dining room drumming his hands on the silver tops of the Christofle carving tables—should have been the crowning moment of Soulé's career. Instead, the moment was marked by a walkout of the entire Kennedy clan. Even more serious than the loss of the Kennedys' patronage, personally more hurtful, financially potentially devastating and most clearly reflecting the changing face of American gastronomy as it evolved, were whispered charges of anti-Semitism.

The accusation dates to 1957 and involved (what else could it be?) the allocation of tables. Soulé dressed a room; not just anyone could be sat at *la Royale*. His landlord, adding nothing to the vital mix that Soulé fashioned daily, was led to a less-than-prominent table whenever he came to eat. Unfortunately for Henri *"Le restaurant c'est moi"* Soulé, his landlord was Harry "I don't get ulcers I give 'em" Cohn, the head of Columbia Pictures. One day, after Mr. Cohn found himself yet again not being led to the sort of table he thought he was entitled to, he more than doubled the yearly rent and charged anti-Semitism.

Now, Mr. Cohn was not someone whom the Anti-Defamation League would necessarily have come running to aid. When asked by fellow film mogul Sam Warner to contribute to the Jewish Relief Fund during World War II, he reportedly answered, "Relief for the Jews! What we need is relief from the Jews!" Still, for Henri Soulé, the charge stuck. Rather than pay the new rent, he moved Le Pavillon to the Ritz Towers at Park Avenue and Fifty-seventh Street. ("This is the last thing I do," he told *Newsweek*. "I do it only for my boys.") However, the very next year, after Harry Cohn died, he was offered his old location back. He couldn't very well move Le Pavillon again, so instead he built a monument to the nostalgia that Joseph Wechsberg had detected in him in his 1953 profile. He had panels painted of the curved bay of St-Jean-de-Luz, the village that is on the same coast as Biarritz, where he had done his apprenticeship, and not far from his native Saubrigues. He called the new restaurant La Côte Basque.

What is being mistaken for anti-Semitism in the Cohn affair is, in fact, snobbery. What Soulé objected to in Cohn was not that he was a Jew but, as Truman Capote wrote in his retelling of the event, that he was a "shoulder-padded counter-jumper." Ludwig Bemelmans (never accused of being an anti-Semite) could quite breezily write of the scenes he'd observed at Jewish weddings while he was a waiter at the Ritz-Carlton. Here was the disheveled grandfather, in a "skullcap," wandering into the kitchen where the busy chef muttered, *"Qu'est-ce qu'il veut ici, ce phénomène?"* There was the overbearing wife instructing her husband not to overeat. "You know what happened last time, Sam. You'll get sick to your stomach. Remember how sick you was? You'll take a physic when I get you home." That Sam's purgative methods were considered not the ideal conversation topic to have one table over from Edward and Mrs. Simpson not only made sense to Soulé, but to avoid it at all costs he thought the responsibility of anyone who considered the most sophisticated level of French gastronomy to be their heritage.

The evidence of anti-Semitism in Soulé is even weaker when looked at in the light of some of Soulé's personal relationships. It is doubtful that the great statesman Bernard Baruch—so conscious of *his* heritage that even late in life, when he was counselor to presidents and friend of Winston Churchill, he could not forget that at university, he'd been denied membership in a Greek letter fraternity because he was Jewish—would actually take an apartment at the Ritz Towers to be closer to the new Pavillon. It is positively certain that Joseph Wechsberg, who coauthored a book with Simon Wiesenthal and whose own mother perished at Auschwitz, would not have had much interest in tracing Soulé's own brand of alienation if he'd suspected him of that same prejudice.

Anti-Semitism is, in fact, the wrong interpretation of a mistrust that Soulé might actually have had. The mistrust of the verbally quick by someone for whom English was a shaky second language, of a "Let's do business" approach by someone for whom the restaurant business was a calling. If Soulé embodied one, a group of people (centered around Beard) who bought and sold from each other, did each other favors, and helped with each other's cooking lessons and promotions embodied the other. It might be called an early version of the food world and it was a world to which, doubtlessly because he believed he towered over it, Soulé did not belong.

A scene that took place occasionally at the bar of the Carlton House Hotel on Madison Avenue illustrates the size of the food and wine world in the mid 1950s and the interconnections that made it up. If you were to spot the three men sitting at a table in the bar, you might have assumed, since they had no other shared visible characteristics, that they were a group of old friends. That they were—they were also three of the most important men in the American wine business. Frank Schoonmaker, an importer and the dean of American wine experts, would invariably be drinking Scotch. Alexis Lichine, described by Wechsberg in the inevitable *New Yorker* profile (1958) as "slow-sipping, fast-talking," would be wearing a Savile Row gray-flannel suit while holding forth on his latest bus trip to someplace like Akron, Ohio, to speak before the local Rotary Club on the subject of wine. Sam Aaron, meanwhile (the owner with his brother Jack of Sherry Wine and Spirits across Madison Avenue from the Carlton House), would have his eyeglasses propped on top of his head, an overflowing ashtray in front of him, and would counter Schoonmaker's encyclopedic knowledge and Lichine's urbanity with his own brand of New York smarts. For him, wine was judged not only by the subtlety of its bouquet, but also by the state of the dollar.

James Beard knew all three well. (At times too well: "Alexis heard that I was going to Germany with Frank and was worried over that. Jesus, there are as many prima donnas in the wine business as there are in any other," he wrote in a 1958 letter.) Beard was promoting the wines of Schoonmaker and Lichine at the Four Seasons and had actually worked for the Aaron brothers—such was the minuscule cast of characters that made up the food world at the time.

Beard's connection to the Aarons went back the farthest, to the mid-1940s and a period between jobs when he was still trying to cobble a career together and they offered him a position as a part-time salesclerk. So began a relationship that developed into Beard becoming an occasional adviser and copywriter for the Aaron brothers and a lifelong friend. The Aarons saw in Beard a fairly unique combination of someone who was knowledgeable, enthusiastic, polished, and did not think himself above "moving cases." Beard in turn saw in the Aarons a similarly singular mix of people who managed to be in the wine business and not indulge in the slightest semblance of European airs.

They would not have wasted their time deluding themselves. The Aarons' start in the wine and spirit business went straight back to Prohibition. In the free-floating spirit of the time, Jack Aaron, then a dock boss, became friendly with Charlie Berns of the speakeasy known as Jack and Charlie's (later "21"). Berns soon realized that Aaron had a gift—priceless in Prohibition. He could distinguish real Scotch from the bathtub variety, which allowed Jack Aaron to transform himself from a dock boss to someone who had regular liquor accounts. Jack Aaron was known for being a bootlegger with principles and for never profiteering in the retail end. His customers appreciated it and when, after repeal in 1933, he bought Sherry Wine and Spirits (not yet called Sherry-Lehman) on Madison Avenue, those same customers became a faithful clientele.

It was his younger brother Sam who would be in charge of the wine end of the store. A trained psychologist, he couldn't find a job in 1934 when he graduated from City College and so went into business with his brother. Quickly tiring of a trade that was comprised almost entirely of liquor sales, in 1935 he saw an opportunity to broaden the minuscule wine selection the store carried when Loeser's department store in Brooklyn dumped their entire wine inventory. Three hundred cases of mixed vintages were for sale, not least of which were the Mouton-Rothschild '28 and Latour '29. The Aarons took a gamble and bought it all. These were roots that Sam Aaron would never forget. For every Château Mouton-Rothschild in Pauillac, he knew there was a Loeser's department store in Brooklyn that was closing it out; for every person looking for something "massive" in a double magnum, there were five hundred looking for something drinkable in a sixty-seven-ounce jug.

Though they were technically in the wine business, they would never have considered themselves experts. Then, in 1937, Frank Schoonmaker came into the store to write them up in his "Roving Reporter" column for the *New Yorker*. He sensed a wine convert in Sam Aaron and invited him to accompany him on a buying trip to France. That, as Sam Aaron would recall years later, "changed the future for the shop and for us."

Aaron could not have hoped for a better teacher. As a travel writer and, later, with Harold Ross's encouragement, a wine writer and, later still, a wine importer, Schoonmaker understood both the world that European wine came from and the constraints of selling it in the United States. Before repeal, his articles had to carry disclaimers such as this one from *House and Garden*: "This article is published in anticipation of the virtual certain repeal of the 18th Amendment and should not be construed as an inducement to our readers to purchase beverages the sale of which is prohibited." After repeal, he was kept busy countering all the idiocy about wine put out by a mass of instant experts whom he described as "a bevy of ladies stating, no doubt with the best intentions in the world that 'Montrachet is one of the better Chablis' (it is, of course, not a Chablis at all), that it is wrong to drink wine with any dish that has been prepared with wine (what is one expected to drink with such dishes?), and that claret glasses resemble baby tumblers." In a country where books on wine often did not go too far beyond being pronunciation manuals— "Château—(sha-to)"—he would go on to write the seminal *American Wines* (1941) and *Frank Schoonmaker's Encyclopedia of Wine* (1964). In the interrelated ways of the food and wine worlds, he was also the first person to take Craig Claiborne to Le Pavillon (where they ate a meal that was a testament to French simplicity: rice pilaf with mussels, tournedos Rossini, salad, Brie, and *oeufs à la neige*, or poached meringue with custard sauce, while drinking a bottle of Montrachet and one of La Tâche) and, in his capacity as a wine importer, an early employer of Alexis Lichine.

In the two-part *New Yorker* profile of Lichine, Wechsberg described him as "a Moscow-born, Paris-reared naturalized-American." Lichine was indeed the perfect vehicle through which Wechsberg was able to play up some of the humor inherent in the American wine business, where the weight of European tradition was brought face-to-face with the power of the American market. While someone like Beebe would always push the tradition (calling the Chevaliers du Tastevin—a group started in 1934 to promote the drinking of Burgundy wine by having its members dress up in medieval-looking costumes— "one of the oldest orders of Knighthood in Christendom"), Wechsberg would always push the American angle. On his bus trips to talk before chamber of commerce groups around the country, Lichine was "a viticultural Billy Graham." When he was giving a biting dissection of the wine list at Antoine's in New Orleans (only to then push his own imports on the owner), he was a practitioner of "a distinctively suave version of the hard sell."

And the hard buy. On the buying trip through Burgundy on which Wechsberg accompanied Lichine, he describes Lichine's hulking late-model Oldsmobile pulling into a farmyard in the tiny village of Chassagne-Montrachet and Lichine's anticipation of the bargaining duel that is about to take place with the famed producer Claude Ramonet over some barrels of his Les Ruchottes. "Claude will tell us that he's got almost nothing to sell," Lichine explains to Wechsberg, "but the difference between almost nothing and nothing can be considerable. There'll be some tremendous haggling—you'll see—and after the sale Claude will be unhappy. To these people selling their wine is like seeing their children leave home."

Thinking of wine as one's child showed a level of sensitivity to the product that was doubtlessly never reached by American importers such as Capitol, which could trace its beginnings to a business venture between Bugsy Siegel and Lucky Luciano. Even with repeal, there were a few conceptual differences between how the wine business was practiced in France and in the United States. In France, the Institut National des Appellations d'Origine made sure that one beautiful village's wines didn't get sold under the name of another. In the United States, the Bureau of Alcohol, Tobacco and Firearms kept an eye on state lines and any potential felonies or bloodbaths that might arise from their crossing. A shipment of wine leaving the hallowed ground of Bordeaux's Quai des Chartrons might well be considered part of the venerable "wine trade," but once it had made it to the warehouses of Long Island City, it was definitely part of what Wechsberg delightedly quoted Lichine as calling "the wine end of the whiskey business."

No one synthesized these disparate influences better than Sam Aaron, and the way he chose to do it was through his own Jewish humor. It wasn't the sort of humor that involves camels or Miami Beach ("I knew he was a male," the retiree tells the policeman taking the report of the lost camel, "because whenever I rode him, people would say 'Look at the schmuck on that camel'"). Nor was it the kind that delights in wordplay: Rue de la Payes for Rue de la Paix.

The kind of Jewish humor that Sam Aaron brought to the wine business was the self-deprecating kind. In later years, when he'd take a suite at the Hôtel de Crillon on the Place de la Concorde and receive the great château owners of France looking for a little shelf space on Madison Avenue, he liked to say, "For a Jewish boy from Brooklyn to be mixed up with the Rothschilds, well, it's amusing."

Nowhere was this clearer than in the catalogue that he soon started to publish five times a year (and which James Beard often contributed to) and which managed, while announcing the season's specials, to playfully deflate some of the social ambitions that often came with a knowledge of wine. The winter 1963 issue, with the theme of skiing, manages to plug RA's Brasserie (diners photographed coming out onto Fifty-third Street with their skis), promote the usual "As we got to press" specials, hawk Back Bay gin and vodka (which, even though they are the aristocratically Bostonian "drinks of Stowe and North Conway," are a nicely proletarian $4.29 a quart), and, in the section devoted to Swiss wines, crack up the attentive reader with a comparison between the skiing conditions to be found in St. Moritz and those to be found in Van Cortlandt Park in the Bronx.

St. Moritz Ski Center.
How reached: Board Swissair 6 P.M. Idlewild, arriving at Zurich 7:25 A.M.

Van Cortlandt Park Ski Center.
How reached: 7th Avenue Broadway Line to 242nd Street and 8-minute walk to ski center . . .

After-ski Activities—St. Moritz: The Palace Hotel . . .

After-ski Activities—Van Cortlandt Park: Subway . . .

I stress the humor because there was something deeply humorless about the whole situation. Sam Aaron may have been mixed up with the Rothschilds, but as late as 1954, James Beard was irritated enough that a Jew was not welcome at the San Francisco chapter of the Wine and Food Society to note it in a letter. How better to deal with it than to tweak some of the pretensions that surrounded the world of European wines, as Sam Aaron did, both in his catalogue and as co-author with James Beard of *How to Eat Better for Less Money*. Here, in his role of consumer advocate for the carriage trade, he let the reader in on little-known secrets, such as that the Napoleon sign the French are given to put on cognac bottles has "no significance whatever, but merely creates and aura of antiquity." That one should return a bad bottle of wine to a wine merchant: "After all, *he* can return the defective bottle to the supplier." And he clearly understood that alcohol wasn't always consumed for its civilizing effect, but often just to get a buzz: "Remember," he wrote on the subject of vodka, "you can always add 25 per cent water to the 100 proof liquor and get the same result as with the 80 proof."

In somewhat the same vein of reality-based marketing, Sam Aaron saw the cross-promotional values of restaurants in selling wine. Two relatively unknown wines for which he was interested in creating a clientele were Château Pétrus, the now legendary wine from Pomerol, and the country wines of the Beaujolais region just north of Lyons. For both of these he chose restaurants whose image corresponded to that of the wine. Thus, for Pétrus—to the great profitability of everyone involved—he came to a "You do it in the restaurant, I'll do it in retail" arrangement with Soulé (whose house wines were Château Simard and Château L'Angélus of Saint-Émilion because Americans found them easy to pronounce). For the 1963 promotion of Beaujolais, the window display at Sherry brought together many of the marketing methods that Sam Aaron used. Against a backdrop of Ballantine's gift boxes, the "James Beard Wine Rack" was stocked with bottles of Beaujolais (a small version of the wine rack was given to anyone who bought a case at Sherry, made to fit into most New York City apartment dwellers' cellar: the closet). Above the display was a picture of the restaurant that was cosponsoring the promotion, Lutèce. Above this picture was another, of the restaurant's owner, André Surmain, wearing a white tie and tails, which undoubtedly were meant to present him as a member of the French nobility, and which, in many ways, were a symbol of the personal self-invention that had gone into the restaurant's founding.

The tiny zinc bar at Lutèce on Fiftieth Street is stamped with the name and address of the company that manufactured it. The address is on the Boulevard Richard-Lenoir, the slightly desolate Parisian boulevard that stems off from the Place de la Bastille on the east side of Paris. To the left of the bar is a small painting of the tiny Place de Furstenberg that is in the heart of the Left Bank. At Lutèce, one has always been able to convince oneself that one has happened on a very happy corner of France. Madame Soltner's warm greeting together with Chef Soltner's cooking made it for decades not only one of the best French restaurants in the country but prototypically French. But the story of how the restaurant opened in 1961 is a story that contains many of the social changes that would roil the restaurant business throughout the decade. Those changes are embodied by the man who originally hired André Soltner to be the chef and from whom Soltner bought the restaurant in 1972, André Surmain.

Grande dame that Lutèce is today, it was initially a creation of Surmain's fevered imagination. It was a personal quality that was apparent even before he went into the restaurant business, when he was still a young man in the food PR business. A typical Surmain promotion might be the one for the New Bedford scallop fleet, when he started a "Miss Scallop" pageant and the winner got to wear a "Miss Scallop" sash. Or else the one for O'Quin Charcoal Sauce ("Bing Crosby's favorite"), in which he drove his Volkswagen van around the New York suburbs with models dressed as characters from *Gone With the Wind* giving away samples. Sales needed an event and, as illogical as some of them may have been, Surmain provided them.

That was a busy little van. By the late 1950s, it had been transformed into an airline-catering vehicle. Air travel at the time essentially covered the same key demographic that the restaurant business was looking for. American Airlines had the "21" flight between New York and Los Angeles, RA had its copywriters churning out witty ads for its airport locations ("It must be a good restaurant, look at all the planes parked outside"), and André Surmain had the Varig and Aeronaves Mexicanas catering accounts. Here the printed menus had cooking tips, the onboard liquor was "21" Brands, and at mealtimes the stewards dressed up as chefs and pretended to carve meat in the cabins.

If organizing this was not enough for Surmain, at the same time he used the proceeds from the sale of his parents' cosmetics company to buy the town house on Fiftieth Street that would eventually become Lutèce. He installed his family on the third floor and a cooking school on the second. Not just any cooking school. Frank Schoonmaker and Alexis Lichine gave classes on wine, Albert Stockli on cooking, and James Beard, of course, was the main instructor. As impressive as the faculty may have been, there was a certain extemporaneous air to the undertaking; one that Surmain was quick to illustrate many year later when I sat down with him one afternoon on the terrace of his restaurant on the square of Mougins in Provence. "Ah, Jim," he said, sipping at his flute of champagne. "We used to go out to do carving demonstrations for ladies' groups in New Jersey. He'd be reading instructions to me while I drove and then we'd do it and come back and split the fee."

I had come to Mougins from London specifically to meet Surmain. It was late October. As the plane descended for the arrival into Nice, I could see the gilded coast from Monte Carlo to Antibes. When I got my rental car, I drove west on the highway in what seemed to be a phalanx of black Ferraris going in the direction of Cannes. I knew I had to ask Surmain a rather indelicate question, one that on the face of it had nothing to do with the restaurant business: Why had he changed his name from Andrew Sussman? The question had a personal angle. On my father's side, I came from a family that had managed to ignore its Jewish heritage for several generations, and because of that, I had a heightened interest in how others had dealt with their Jewish background. Maybe, after all, it did have something to do with the restaurant business. Anglicizing one's Jewish name was practically an American tradition, but Francocizing it took it one step farther. Had Surmain felt in 1961 that he had to have a French name to own a French restaurant?

Before I reached Cannes, I turned up into the hills and drove into Mougins. I tracked Surmain down at his restaurant on the village square. The trellis in the dining room seemed like a direct reference to the original decor of Lutèce. He had short-cropped hair, high cheekbones, the stance of a polo player at rest, and wore an old chef's jacket frayed at the cuffs. We sat down on the terrace and almost immediately I posed the question about his name change. "That old canard," he said, laughing. "Yes, I'm a Jew, but I changed my name long before I went into the restaurant business, during the war, when I was in the OSS. In case I was captured."

There was something delightfully roguish about the way he answered; a glimpse, I thought, of the theatrical nature of the food business of the late 1950s and early 1960s, one that Surmain with his "Miss Scallop" pageants and stewards dressed as chefs was so adept at staging. It was an ability that was not lost on American Airlines, who, in seeing his success with smaller airlines, soon asked him to take over their entire catering operation. This was major. This was more than one little Volkswagen van could handle. He knew that he'd be out of his depth with the logistics and his talents for showmanship would be lost in the sheer volume of the operation. Surmain turned down American Airlines and instead decided to combine his experience and his natural talents and open a restaurant.

He borrowed $50,000 from one-time Mexican president Miguel Alemán, whom he had gotten to know by catering the national airline, and another $50,000 from Bankers Trust. He had the name he wanted. He had the town house. All he needed was the chef. He flew to Paris, treated himself to the Hôtel Le Bristol, and looked up a young cook named André Soltner who was a friend of a pastry chef who'd done catering with him. Soltner was working at an Alsatian brasserie in Montparnasse called Chez Hansi. Surmain went to eat there and after the meal introduced himself to Soltner and explained that he was looking for a chef for the restaurant he was about to open in New York. The next day, Soltner drove his Deux-Chevaux over to the Rue du Faubourg Saint-Honoré to show Surmain the tallow (sheep's fat mixed with wax) sculptures that he'd made and which were, at the time, proof of professional artistry in a French chef. Surmain was suitably impressed—they had a deal.

Back in New York, they put up their painting of the Place de Furstenberg, they installed the zinc bar, they placed two Parisian street lamps outside the front door, and they opened for business on February 16, 1961. It was, indeed, a little corner of France, and it was welcomed as such by the growing number of New Yorkers eager to experience an authentic French restaurant. There were, however, certain aspects of early Lutèce that Soulé, a less forgiving critic than most, would not necessarily have approved of. And it wasn't just the mismatched silver.

One wonders, though not for long, what Soulé might have said when the customers eating in the second-floor dining room heard the Surmains' daughter rollerskating along the corridor of their third-floor home. One can only imagine the expression on Soulé's face had he ever seen Surmain in his rust-colored Hush Puppies wrestling with a swimming pool cover above the patio during summer thunderstorms.

As shocked as he might have been, he could not have failed to see that the place was full. There was something fresh about it that the customers enjoyed. The total un-Souléness of it all. At Lutèce the selling never stopped. There wasn't a promotion that they wouldn't do. When portable TVs first came out, Surmain allowed the manufacturer to place one on every table for a night. When Swanson Frozen Dinners wanted to improve its image, it had a pretty model photographed in the kitchen taking one of its meals out of an oven. (It must be said for the record that in the photograph of this scene that Surmain showed me, André Soltner looks very close to losing his Alsatian sang-froid.)

But what would have displeased Soulé most was the breezily insouciant attitude that Surmain had toward the tenets of class. "We were really elegant," Surmain told me in Mougins, "high WASP." Then, in case I was unsure as to what this social class might look like, he added, "You know, blazers."

"Did you ever meet Soulé?" I asked him.

"Almost," he said with a grin. "I went to eat at Le Pavillon. He expected me to come over and greet him. I was the customer and I expected him to come over and greet me. So we didn't speak."

The long afternoon in Mougins had turned into night. The square had emptied. We polished off our flutes of champagne and I thanked Surmain for his time. We shook hands and I started back toward my hotel. The lights of hamlets shone across the valley looking north toward Grasse. I thought of Soulé's silence when faced with Surmain. It could not have been good news to him that someone running a supposedly elegant restaurant could put portable televisions on the tables and still be successful. Could he sense already that the American dining public had reached the stage in its relationship to France that it could take the food but leave the attitude? Could he, in fact, sense what the future held?

THE LAST DAYS OF HAUTE CUISINE

Henri Soulé defined himself by strikes. It was as if he needed work stoppages by his staff to make real for him the constraints of trying to run a great French restaurant in the United States. Already by 1945, four years after opening, the waiters were picketing in front of Le Pavillon. Their demand was that they not be forced to work the same stations in the dining room, the way that Soulé insisted they do. He wanted them to know each regular customer's tastes; they wanted to have rotation established so they would all get an opportunity to work the dining room stations that tipped the most. Since they weren't prepared to pool their tips, it led to a strike. It was an event. "The Talk of the Town" wanted to know what Lucius Beebe ate. *P.M.* magazine wanted photos of the ermine-wrapped picket breakers. The waiters were indiscreet: "That Cole Porter is a fussy one," one of them allowed. Soulé quickly realized that what he was trying to do was provide butler, not waiter, service to his best customers and that, in this country, was impossible to do. By the time of the 1960 walkout of Le Pavillon's kitchen staff, the innocence of the earlier strike was gone. At issue were Soulé's conflicting demands that the standards be maintained and that the hours the staff worked be cut. In fifteen years, the economic survival problems had gone from being the waiters' to being Soulé's.

He did not help himself by insisting that "Russian service" be maintained. Proud as chefs were at the level of workmanship they could display on the platters that were presented tableside, they were also aware of the implications such service held for their food cost. At its strictest interpretation, service "à la Russe" demanded that if a chicken or duck was ordered, the whole bird had to be presented. Similarly with the cakes that were put on the dessert cart. If one slice was sold at lunch, the whole cake had to be replaced for dinner. Soulé would never begin a service with a cake that had been cut into. The result was that the staff meal invariably consisted of leftover chicken and cake. But the perils of such service didn't end there. As the financial situation deteriorated, Soulé suspected his captains of "carving thick" to get bigger tips and to counter them he sent up his most trusted sous-chef, Roger Fessaguet, to do the dining room carving himself. Having a cook in the dining room was Soulé's idea of adapting.

The one variable that Soulé could reduce was his labor cost, and in 1960 he instructed his chef, Pierre Franey, to cut the hours the kitchen staff worked to thirty-five per week. Franey refused, insisting that at those hours he simply could not maintain the standards of Le Pavillon. Together with Jacques Pépin and six other members of the brigade he walked out, heading to Forty-eighth Street between Eighth and Ninth Avenues, the location of the Vatel Club. This was the French chef's social club that was named after Vatel, the majordomo of the Prince de Condé, who had stood on principle and impaled himself on a sword when the fish for a banquet for Louis XIV threatened to arrive late. Clearly, when they felt they had to, the French could go all the way.

Claiborne heard what had happened. He rushed over to the club and was filled in on the details of the "speechless fight." The headline over his story in the next day's paper read "Le Pavillon Shut in Gallic Pique." "If I do it, my men quit on me," Franey told *Time*. "They are underpaid, getting the minimum. You can not shave an egg. It has no hair." "He was like a son to me," Soulé countered. "But now M. Franey is a fresh little man." Snits, huffs, walkouts, recriminations and principled stances, things were starting to get very French and very volatile. All it took to ignite them further was the subject of American presidential politics.

L'Affaire Kennedy was a clash of gigantic egos, Soulé's and Joe Kennedy's. It started when Soulé overheard Kennedy telling the Pavillon's maître d', Fred Decré, "Fred, you're an American, why are you working for that lousy Frenchman?" It was advice that Decré would eventually take when together with La Côte Basque director, Robert Meyzen, and Roger Fessaguet they opened La Caravelle in 1960. It was located on Fifty-fifth Street, as was Soulé's La Côte Basque, but just west enough of Fifth Avenue for Soulé, ever forgiving, to refer to them from that day on as "the busboys from the west side."

As a means of avenging himself on Kennedy, Soulé found himself being asked in the middle of a crowded dining room—in what smells like a setup—whether he thought John Kennedy had a chance of ever being elected president. "Not a chance, not a chance," he answered loudly enough for the whole dining room to hear.

The next move was Kennedy's. One day shortly after Soulé's political analysis, the Kennedys were eating *en famille* when Mr. Joe spotted a photographer who was taking pictures inside. Having the hope of the Democratic Party photographed eating in one of the most expensive restaurants in the country was something that Mr. Joe wanted to avoid. Truly as if he owned the restaurant (it has always been suspected that Kennedy bankrolled Soulé in 1941, which might explain their neurotic attachment), he summoned Soulé. He came to Le Pavillon to eat and not to be photographed, he barked, and ordered Soulé to immediately have the photographer thrown out.

Now, there is one rule that applies to all French restaurants, whatever their standard, whether in a truck driver's *routier* or a *Michelin* three-star. It is not—as anyone who has ever sent a dish back in a French restaurant knows—"The customer is always right," but rather "You don't tell the *patron* how to run his business." And so, while we do know that Soulé muttered something in French about how Kennedy's son was not yet elected president and already he was acting like a dictator, we don't know the subtleties of the Gallic shrug with which the answer was surely accompanied. Was it the slightly apologetic raising of the shoulders that a French post office clerk might offer, signaling that matters are out of their control? Or was it the vaguely affronted shrug that, together with palms held stiffly outward, signals that a Frenchman is nearing his emotional threshold. Or did Soulé actually find it necessary to employ the full shrug, which at its most perfected levels is performed with a pursed lip refinement that can only be effectively translated as "Screw you!"

In any case, it was the photographer who stayed and the Kennedys who got up *en famille*—*en clan*—and left. From that day on, La Caravelle became their New York restaurant. When John Kennedy was elected president and a young sous-chef from the Essex House, René Verdon, was chosen to be White House chef, he went to train under Roger Fessaguet in the subterranean kitchens at La Caravelle. Some of the large-hotel chefs in New York let it be known that Verdon could never actually get such a plum job because he was not, like them, a Freemason, the semisecret fraternity to which many French chefs belong. Fessaguet—who had arrived in the United States at the age of seventeen thirteen years previously—answered that not being a Freemason would not present a problem for Verdon because Fessaguet happened to know for a fact that neither was the president of the United States.

A new spirit was in the air, one that in order to understand we have to turn once again to Lucius Beebe. "There is a fugitive feeling among Republicans and responsible people generally," he had written in the *San Francisco Chronicle* in 1960, "that it may have been a good thing for everybody if Stevenson had been the Democratic nominee instead of a rich mick from the Boston lace curtain district." It may be pertinent to note that at the time he wrote this, he was living in Nevada in a private train with a reproduction of the Sistine Chapel's ceiling painted overhead. As well as he may have understood the Jazz Age, Camelot seems to have escaped him. He was still selling class distinctions, but fewer and fewer people were buying.

As dear as the sentiments expressed by Beebe may have been to Soulé, someone in his current financial position could not afford to be quite as high-handed. As proof that he was prepared to adapt—further than he had ever imagined—in 1961, when RA announced that they were taking the company public, Soulé contacted them and informed them that he was prepared to join his restaurants to theirs in a publicly held company.

The phone call came as a surprise to Jerry Brody. He knew that Soulé had threatened to fire Pierre Franey if he even set foot in the Four Seasons. Why would he want to go into business with them? But he didn't dismiss the suggestion immediately. He had too much respect for Soulé. Many years later, Brody described to me his favorite Soulé memory: "I was having dinner at Le Pavillon and the man who owned the company that did all our linens was having dinner there also. At one stage he started coming over to greet me and Soulé intercepted him. 'But do you know who's here?' the man started. 'Soulé is here,' he said and sat the man back down." To be in such total control of a dining room and one's customers' dining experience as to thwart even the possibility of them having to respond to an unwelcome greeting was undoubtedly a beautiful thing to experience. But it had its price. Soon after receiving Soulé's phone call, Brody went over to Le Pavillon one afternoon between services and over a bottle of pink champagne and a tin of caviar he studied Soulé's books. "Only Le Pavillon was making some money," Brody recalled. But not enough. In 1961, RA turned Henri Soulé down.

⬌

THE FORMIDABLE
MRS. CHILD

Clearly on the ascendant, as Soulé was on the descendant, in December 1962, RA hosted, at the Four Seasons, the thirty-eighth annual dinner of the American chapter of the Confrérie des Chevaliers du Tastevin. Among the courses that Albert Stockli served were *truites du lac farcies à la crème de porto* (an adaptation of Fernand Point's *truite au porto*), *tourte feuilletée aux cailles*, and *pyramides de bœuf tastevin*. *Look* magazine, which was covering the event for a later issue, described the atmosphere as one of "whimsical court pageantry." Nowhere was this more apparent than during the serving of the *pièce de résistance*, which was performed by "red-leotarded tumblers, with ox-masks, who ran from all the doors of the dining room to form a three-tier human pyramid." In other words, another typically understated RA production.

Presiding over this feast was, in his role of *commandeur*, the publisher Alfred A. Knopf and, in his role of *grand sénéchal*, the president of Chanel, Gregory Thomas. Thomas was a man who showed a touching eagerness to join any gastronomic society: he was not only *grand sénéchal* of the Confrérie but also *grand maître* of the Commanderie de Bordeaux, *chevalier* of the Confrérie de la Chaîne des Rôtisseurs, member of the Amis d'Escoffier, *commandeur* of the Commanderie des Cordons Bleus, and *grande langouste* of Les Langoustes.

That these much-esteemed gastronomes had chosen the Four Seasons to hold their dinner was going to have a huge legitimizing effect on the restaurant's reputation. Between courses, Joe Baum paced in the corridor like a father-to-be. In the kitchen, James Beard kept out of the way and sat on Albert Stockli's desk. ("It was perfection to the last bit," he would later report to Helen Evans Brown, "with a few fucks and shits thrown around by Albert and with good reason.") Sitting beside Beard on Stockli's desk was a six-foot-tall woman who occasionally got up to watch the *pièces montées* paraded around the dining room and, according to Beard, "came back in tears." The previous year her cookbook *Mastering the Art of French Cooking* had been published to great success by Commandeur Knopf's house—Julia Child.

There are several levels of irony to this scene. The first is the very fact that with RA's guileless ability to mix genres "medieval court pageantry" was being held in a Mies van der Rohe building. The second is the sheer power of the names present—Baum, Beard, Child, among others—made the Four Seasons, on this particular night, the very center of the American food world less than ten years after they opened their first tablecloth restaurant. The third is the very fact of a Chevaliers dinner being held in the corporate headquarters of a company that during Prohibition had on occasion showed a certain disregard for federal laws that prohibited the importation of alcohol. The fourth is less historical but perhaps more telling. If preparing the meal hadn't been hard enough, *Look* informed its readers that toward the end of the article they would find the recipes "adapted for exceptional home dining by director-chef Albert Stockli."

That the average *Look* reader might attempt stuffed trout après Point, the puff pastry quail heads of the *tourte feuilletée*, or, unimaginably, the *pyramides de bœuf tastevin* is indicative of the hunger that existed in this country for the right way to entertain. The pursuit of gastronomy in this country was about to be transformed. No longer would it be the domain of the *grande langouste* but rather that of the frantic hostess in a Pucci caftan mopping at the flop sweat as she peered through the Pyrex oven door to see if the *soufflé aux crevettes* was rising. To help in this transition, someone very special was needed, someone who could both understand the elite art of gastronomy and communicate it through the mass medium of television. The tall woman sitting beside Beard was that person. Slightly over a month after the dinner at the Four Seasons, on January 23, 1963, Julia Child walked into an auditorium at the Boston Gas Company for the taping of the first of thirteen episodes of *The French Chef*, which Boston station WGBH had agreed to run and, in a moment that today seems preordained, she faced the television camera and started talking.

It was a moment that almost didn't happen. If *Mastering the Art of French Cooking* hadn't been published, it never would have. What put the book in danger of not being published was that publishers thought its approach, tellingly, too thorough. Too much about French food and not enough about France. Julia Child would have none of that. "We are heartily sick of the 'charm school,'" Child, speaking for herself and her two co-authors Simone Beck and Louisette Bertholle, wrote to a potential publisher in 1952. "We are tired of Grandmere and Tante Marie and the dear old 'patron' who sits down at your table."

This approach did not sound like a good idea at all to the New York publisher Ives Washburn, Inc., who quickly turned down the unfinished book. Houghton Mifflin would do the same, though the book was closer to completion by the time they received it and they, above all, were frightened by the production costs of the massive manuscript. The rejection letter was accompanied by the suggestion from the editor Dorothy de Santillana that they send it on to Knopf; with the caveat that books on French cooking were more likely to be accepted if they were written by French chefs than by American women. She was right. To have any chance of success in the U.S. market the sales department would indeed want the oversimplified recipes of a nice big chef in a great big toque and not ones that were both detailed and lacking a Tante Marie component. In an undated letter to Beck and Child's friend and publishing mentor, Avis DeVoto, Child wrote, "We must accept the fact that this may well be a book unacceptable by any publisher, as it requires work on the part of the reader."

Reading the Child-DeVoto correspondence at the Schlesinger Library in Radcliffe in Cambridge, Massachusetts (under the watchful eye of the graduate students who work as part-time librarians), one has three very different facets of Julia Child's personality jumbled together in the same manila folder. The first is the one that doggedly pursues publishing possibilities in a saga that spans almost a decade. The second aspect (which can have one stifling chuckles in the Schlesinger's manuscript reading room) is one in which we are constantly reminded of the sheer esprit of her personality, which has made generations of Americans feel as if they actually know her. "Last week 'Alle Kvinners Blad' (Everywoman's Weekly) came here for an interview," she wrote from husband Paul's posting in Norway in early 1961, "and I stupidly conducted it in Norwegian, just because I love to talk Norwegian at any chance I get." An interview by an American author about her forthcoming French cookbook conducted in Norwegian. *Pourquoi-pas?*

But in the same manila folder, in "noteskys" jotted off from Paul's many postings, typed on onionskin paper in the tiny elite type of the portable typewriter, one comes across a third Julia Child, one we wouldn't "know" from television. This Julia Child is politically engaged, particularly on the subject of Senator Joe McCarthy's infamous hunt for a "red menace" in the heart of the U.S. government. "It shows how well the GOP and McCarthy have done their work," she wrote to DeVoto in September 1953. "Just one little old Commie, no matter how insignificant, per every two weeks, and he can keep himself going. I am really getting tired of 'anti Communism.' I retch at the word."

Perhaps one should not be surprised to find such political interest. DeVoto's husband, Bernard, a writer and editor, was considered one of the wise men of the Democratic Party and, closer to home for Child, McCarthy had started his witch-hunt by holding up a list of 205 "communist agents" working in the Department of State, which happened to be Paul Child's employer. And, yet, to have come to the Schlesinger in search of culinary influences and to find political ones is to be made aware that the conditions that go into the writing of a cookbook are as broad as society itself. That it can be as much a cookbook's context as its content that can make it succeed or fail, and that context is as dependent on the newspaper's front page as its cooking page.

On May 5, 1952, Child wrote to DeVoto describing the people joining the tours of Paris that she was then organizing. "We have been to the Folies Bergeres, the Lido, the Ritz Bar, the Meurice Bar, the Tour d'Argent, the Table du Roi and are now taking quite a bit of bicarbonate of soda . . . I don't ever want to go to any of them again . . . And what is worse, a great many of these people are for Taft and think McCarthy is doing a fine thing, which makes digestion even more difficult. What is the country coming to I sometimes wonder."

This is only six months before her letter to Ives Washburn, Inc., strongly stating that the cookbook she and her co-authors were working on would be written without the benefit of the presence of

Grandmere, Tante Marie, or "the dear old 'patron' who sits down at your table." Juxtaposition is a weak argumentative tool and yet one wonders if in the stridency of the second letter there isn't a certain rejection of the people described in the first. To Child, in 1952, the "easy" cookbooks of the period, where it was invariably promised that any great French sauce could be reconstituted out of the ingredients in a kitchen cupboard, may well have been a reflection of the "easy" approach to politics that made someone like McCarthy, with his accusations and unsubstantiated lists, possible.

It wasn't until DeVoto sent the book to Knopf in 1960, where it was taken on by editor Judith Jones, that the originality of the book was recognized. All the factors that had worked against it with other publishers worked for it here. Its Mrs. Beeton–like thoroughness marked it as an epochal cookbook, while its intentional lack of atmospheric color—its Tante Marie-lessness—paradoxically communicated an idea of France more completely than any number of cookbooks with interminable passages about how things were done in France. It was the old writing adage "Show, don't tell" applied to cookbook writing.

Here was the perfectly roasted chicken of the French Sunday table, here were the *petits pois* surely fresh from the garden of the curé, here were the still-warm and slightly caramelized *tartes aux fruits* whose scent alone could conjure up all the poplar-lined roads of France. The book, in fact, was dedicated to *"La Belle France"* and between the instantly recognizable fleur-de-lis covers, and encrypted in the Granjon typeface, this ideal France was lovingly evoked.

"The book is revolutionary," Jones wrote to DeVoto three months before publication. As enthusiastic as she was, she had her reservations about its marketability. "The book is certainly going to need all the push we can possibly give it, particularly with Gourmet coming out this fall with a Louis Diat cookbook." In the very same letter, she also gave a hint of the solution: "Julia Child is, of course, a marvel, and if we can get her out in the stores and on the air she would be our best possible advertisement."

That the forty-eight-year-old wife of a retired cultural attaché with the U.S. Foreign Service would go up against the chef that invented vichyssoise was indeed a risky proposition. But it was that very background that she would put to invaluable use when it came to the book's promotion. Julia Child may not have spent her youth skimming stocks in subterranean kitchens, but she had been to enough boring diplomatic parties to never allow a conversational silence to settle. Thus, on tour in November 1961, she could call radio appearances "interviews with chit-chat" while department store demonstrations were "cooking and chatter," or what Paul described as "making polite noises at the club women." Recently retired, he had become the happy chronicler of a promotional tour for a cookbook that was selling. "So to San Francisco, where the pattern repeats," he wrote to DeVoto, "the buying wave has swept through the city like the river through the Augean stables, leaving dozens of frustrated women behind frantically waving ten dollar bills at hapless clerks in bookstores."

My next employers may have been among the lucky ones who managed to buy the book. There was a well-worn copy kept in the kitchen bookcase. After burning out at "21" I had resurfaced across the country as a private chef in a mansion in Pacific Heights looking out over San Francisco Bay. My employers, an older society couple, had beautiful old-fashioned manners. They never asked for anything to be done by phrasing it in an order. Their way of telling the butler to build a fire was not "Build a fire, please," but rather "I think we'll have a fire tonight." Similarly, the way the lady of the house would tell me, for example, to make a cherry clafouti was to say, "There's such a good recipe for cherry clafouti in Julia Child." I always got a kick out of this because telling your private cook which recipe you wanted made from a book in which the very first words read "This is a book for the servantless American cook" so missed the point of Julia Child.

But the culinary twists that went on in that house didn't end there. The man of the house would always come into the kitchen after dinner to say thank you—a point of politeness that, for me, defined their manners—and on one of those occasions, I took the opportunity of suggesting that to vary the menu from time to time we might try an ethnic dish. I can still see him standing in his monogrammed velvet John Lobb slippers, peering out at the lights twinkling across the bay, at once amused at the pleasure his bon mot was giving him and chagrined that he had to express it. "Patric," he finally said, *"French is as ethnic as I get."* With an epiphanic swiftness, I understood that I was over here now, not over there.

The second twist I got to experience was when I saw what could pass for French food. When an unexpected group showed up one evening—the lights had gone out at a friend's bridge supper before the food had been served—the lady of the house came in to the kitchen and told me to keep it simple: mix some cans of Campbell's split pea and tomato soups, heat this, and add some handfuls of the shrimp we kept in the freezer. I did so. She tasted it, rectified the seasoning with a few splashes of Christian Brothers dry sherry, and with a delighted smile said, "Ah, bisque." For me, it was a pre-Childian moment, a glimpse of the cooking style of another time; but for her I knew it was a cherished recipe that reminded her of another time, another place, perhaps even a younger self, and so I kept it in the rotation of the first courses I would serve them.

The maid, Maria, was a large woman from Guadalajara, Jalisco. She was always in motion, dusting, walking the terriers, darning while casting an eye over the newspaper headlines and saying, *"Patricio, Dios ve todo."* She liked me because I would include in the house order to the grocer the cilantro, serrano chiles, and corn tortillas that she kept in the fridge and because I made sure her *menudo* didn't boil over while she was upstairs making the beds and dusting. But I think she liked me most because every morning I went to the trouble of straining the bacon fat left over from breakfast into an empty tin of Folger's coffee that we kept in the fridge. On her days off, Maria would transport it, on her lap across town on the 22 bus, to her daughter's apartment in the Mission District. Here they sold hog maws in the butchers, plantains in the sidewalk stands; and the ice creams the street vendors served consisted of brightly colored syrups poured over shaved ice. In the cramped kitchen of Maria's daughter's apartment, the bacon from my employers' breakfast became part of the *masa* for tamales. On Sunday evenings, when Maria came back to work, she would bring some of the tamales with her and we'd resteam them and open up the cornhusks and eat them at the staff table looking out at the bay.

If I happened to be serving the house bisque that evening, I went into cognitive overload. French food here was "ethnic" but a mixture of canned American soups exemplified it. Meanwhile, the authentic ethnic dish being consumed in the kitchen had been adapted to American conditions and was made all the tastier, Maria found, by the addition of a by-product of our employers' very English breakfast.

French food was not a style that adapted as successfully. Sometimes I'd look at the plates of bisque come back clean from the dining room and I thought that I could see a whole nation eating it. *Holiday* magazine's 1960 Restaurant Awards tell the sad tale. From La Salle du Bois in Washington, D.C., with its "Fine Gallic Menu," to Les Ambassadeurs at the Diplomat Hotel in Hollywood-by-the-Sea, Florida, with its "Luxurious French Atmosphere," one can almost taste the back flavor of Worcestershire in the amandine and see the corn syrup consistency of the *sauce à l'orange*. There was something parodic about the whole enterprise of haute cuisine in this country, something that by 1963 even its great defender, Craig Claiborne, could no longer deny. In a *New York Times Magazine* article entitled "Along the

Escoffier Circuit," he described some of the low moments that one might expect to have. At the Restaurant Trop Chique one might experience "The Indifferent Captain," "The Same Old Appetizer," "The So-So Chef," and "The Factory Made Pastries." The Trop Chique was indeed a miniature representation of what was going on across the country. Soulé's experiment on whether haute cuisine at its highest level could survive on American soil had seemingly failed. It was all bad bisque. All effect and no substance. All sense and no sensibility. The famed Russian service had become—in thousands of nightly tableside renditions; over Sterno flames not hot enough to sear meat—bad steak Diane.

It was as if French cooking had finally succumbed under all the social aspirations that for so long it had been made carry. A shift in perception was needed to revive it. That shift would occur in California, in the most unlikely of places: across the Bay Bridge from San Francisco, on Shattuck Avenue in Berkeley, in a restaurant with a collective philosophy located in a building that had once been a plumber's store. It had a honeysuckle hedge and a monkey puzzle tree in front and it was called Chez Panisse.

GRILLED

The nineteenth century came to an end in America only in the 1960s...
—Janet Malcolm, *The Silent Woman*

The grotesque prudishness and archness with which garlic is treated in this country has led to the superstition that rubbing the bowl with it before putting the salad in gives sufficient flavour. It rather depends whether you're going to eat the bowl or the salad.
—Elizabeth David, *Summer Cooking*

FROM PERINO'S TO CHEZ PANISSE

There is a stretch of Wilshire Boulevard near the Hancock Park neighborhood of Los Angeles where the passage of time is marked by the state of certain buildings. The Ambassador Hotel anchors this area. Once the home of the famed Cocoanut Grove, today the hotel's windows are shuttered and its legendary landscaping is baked dry and surrounded by barbed wire. Across from the hotel on Wilshire, at what was once the location of the Brown Derby, the hat-shaped restaurant in whose booths Hollywood stars liked to eat their cobb salads, is Brown Derby Plaza, a two-story minimall that has a copy store and a Korean pool hall as tenants. Not far from here (past the Wilshire Temple from where Irving Thalberg was buried in 1936) is Perino's, the massive restaurant, fronted by cypress trees, that was once considered the best in the west.

Perino's is still painted the flamingo-pink shade that (before it was replaced by monastic white-on-white) was the color of Southern California glamour. But it is closed. No cars pull in under the wrought-iron porte cochere any longer. The valet parker's key box, empty now, swings open and shut with every gust of wind. A real estate sign nailed to the wall facing Wilshire gives two different telephone numbers, one for those interested in purchasing the seventeen-thousand-square-foot restaurant, the other for those interested in renting it as a film location. Filming, in fact, is the only reason the restaurant gets opened anymore. The production trucks park in the parking lot, the caterer lays out long tables under the drooping fronds of the untrimmed palm trees, and the extras, wearing the suits and long dresses once required to enter Perino's, sit around in the heat and wait for the head-setted PAs to give them their call.

The ideal mood Perino's aspired to create was one of European sophistication. The sort of compliment the owner, Alexander Perino, wished to hear was "As good as the best in Paris or Rome." It was a transplanted model. (Its most Californian aspect was that it was housed in a building that had once been a Thrifty Supermarket.) It could easily have been one of the California restaurants Joan Didion mentioned in her 1965 essay "Notes from a Native Daughter" as examples of the sort of place where the essence of California was not to be found. "It is very easy to sit at the bar in, say, La Scala in Beverly Hills, or Ernie's in San Francisco," she wrote, "and to share in the pervasive delusion that California is only five hours from New York by air. The truth is that La Scala and Ernie's are only five hours from New York by air. California is somewhere else." With the authority of a native Sacramentan, she went on to explain that the real California existed in a town like Modesto, where a sign over the main street read "Water, Wealth, Contentment, Health."

Driving through California's agricultural and heavily irrigated valleys, past towns such as Soledad and Gonzalez that proudly stamp their names on the water towers that loom over the flat roofs of their settlements, past the eucalyptus windbreaks that separate the fields, past the green swath of crops that follow the beds of rivers like the Pajaro and the Salinas, one comes to appreciate just how right Didion was. The real California exists not in restaurants attempting to reproduce versions of East Coast sophistication, not in reconverted Thrifty Supermarkets on Wilshire Boulevard, but rather out here where water means something.

The town of Hemet in the low desert southeast of Los Angeles is such a town. As one approaches Hemet, the desert scrubland gives way to the usual gauntlet of fast food and car-part franchises and one can easily think one is entering Anytown, U.S.A. But there is a western identity to Hemet. It doesn't come so much from the restored (and reantiquated) downtown saloons but rather from signs driven into the chaparral that surrounds the town, which by giving the phone numbers for well-drilling and cloud-seeding services communicate, with a typical western fervor, how easily this landscape can be transformed.

Much has changed in Hemet over the last sixty years, but the obsession with water is doubtlessly the same as it was in 1940, when an American couple recently evacuated from Europe would sit by their radio on their ranch in the hills above town and find themselves crying as they listened to reports of the fall of Paris. His name was Dillwyn Parrish. He was a painter. Two years previously, because of an embolism caused by Buerger's disease, his right leg had been amputated above the knee. He had one year left to live. Her name was Mary Frances Kennedy Fisher. She had written one cookbook, called *Serve It Forth*, before moving to Hemet, but it was the books written here and—more importantly—the voice forged by what she was about to live through that would play a pivotal role in the culinary transformation of California.

Fisher, the daughter of a newspaper publisher from the dry Quaker town of Whittier in the orange groves east of Los Angeles, had first gone to Europe as the wife of Al Fisher, a doctoral student writing his dissertation on French literature at the University of Dijon. Her early letters home have the breathless tone of a wide-eyed young woman in the full throes of a cultural year abroad and are full of descriptions of lamplighters and hot chestnut sellers and doorways and cathedral windows.

Ten years later, life had seared this tone from her style. She was divorced from Al Fisher and, to please her mother, had gone through the formality of marrying Parrish. They had fled Europe on the *Normandie*—in a truly uncanny coincidence in a crossing four months previous to the one that brought Soulé and his brigade to the New York World's Fair. After traveling west, they were living on a rocky ninety-acre ranch near Hemet in the hills above the Ramona Bowl. Despite the desert air, Parrish's condition seemed only to be worsening. There were futile trips to the Mayo Clinic in Minnesota that led only to amputations farther up on the leg. He was constantly in pain. To dull it, she gave him daily injections of snake venom—because the war had stopped the importation of Analgeticum, the one painkiller that had helped him. To take his mind from it, she wrote and read to him the jaunty book *Consider the Oyster*. None of it worked. In the blazing desert heat of August 1941, Parrish took a gun and shot himself.

She threw herself into work. The first book she wrote after he died was *How to Cook a Wolf*, a cookbook for the war-rationed times. Its recipes involve cans and MSG; its pointers are the many good uses cooking water can be put to. It is as if she was trying to forget herself in practicalities. But it would have been too simple if this had been enough of a response to the cruel death of the love of her life. The book she wrote the year after, published in 1943, *The Gastronomical Me*, showed to what an extent it wasn't enough. If she were to survive her grief she was going to have to get personal. "I tell about myself, and how I ate bread on a lasting hillside, or drank red wine in a room now blown to bits," she wrote in the introduction. Written between a job as a screenwriter at Paramount Studios and return trips to the house in Hemet, formulated in part as a memoir of happy meals by a woman now dining alone, *The Gastronomical Me* is a book by a woman who, like the Europe that she writes about, has herself been blown to bits.

The voice is that of a woman who is fully aware that she is coming apart. Throughout *The Gastronomical Me* she refers to Parrish as Chexbres (pronounced "shebre"), the name of a hamlet above the house overlooking Lake Geneva where they had once been idyllically happy. At the time of writing, she may have still been too grief stricken to even spell out "Timmy," the name by which Parrish was known. "For several months after Chexbres died," she wrote, "I was in flight, not from myself particularly nor of my own volition. I would be working in my little office and suddenly go as fast as I could out the door and up the road, until I had no breath left. Or my sister Anne would look at me and say, judiciously, as if I were a vase of flowers to be moved here and there, 'You must go to Mexico.'"

She did indeed take the journey to Mexico that her sister suggested. So brittle was her state of mind that she spent the night before flying out from Los Angeles riding up and down in the elevator with the Filipino elevator boy eating Life Savers and smoking cigarettes. The next day, on the first leg of the air journey, the passengers were offered for breakfast two "oddly obscene" envelopes. "Perhaps, I needed food," she wrote. "But I thought that those limp cellophane envelopes of hot egg and meat were the most disgusting things I had ever seen." This was not the carping of a jaded air traveler. The objection wasn't that the food lacked flavor, but that to someone in Fisher's emotional state, it lacked life.

The first stopover was in Mazatlán. While the other passengers immediately surrounded the concierge at the hotel, she waited, not particularly caring whether she got a room at all. Before going up to her room, she had a drink at the bar with a man whose impersonality pleased her. Up in the room, she admired that the maids had already laid out her nightgown on the bed with a pinched-in waist, the way the maids had done at the Ritz or at the Trois Couronnes in Vevey. She dressed for dinner. Feeling strong, she sat at the bar with some fellow passengers who she suspected pitied her because she was traveling alone. She ordered tequila and a beer chaser. When it was her turn to buy, she invited them, but they "laughed dryly," and said, "no, no, one was plenty thank you." To their great displeasure—for they thought they were being kind—she turned down their offer to accompany them into town and instead she headed alone into the hotel dining room. She tried to eat again but the food was "abominable . . . a tasteless sopa de pasta, a salad of lukewarm fish and bottled dressing, some pale meat." The waiter, seeing that she had touched none of it—not even the "poudingue inglesa" he brought her for dessert—suddenly leaned toward her, pointed at the kitchen, and whispered how there was both an American kitchen and a country kitchen behind the door. He then disappeared into the kitchen and reappeared with a bowl of the soup that the kitchen workers were eating.

This is the crucial scene, the one that holds the glimmer of personal reconstruction, the moment in which she began to eat again. "The bowl had beans in it," she wrote, "cooked with some tomato and onion and some herbs. I ate them with a big spoon, and now and then rolled up a tortilla from the plate and ate it sopped in the beans.

"And the feeling of that hot strong food going down into my stomach was one of the finest I had ever had. I think it was the first thing I had really tasted since Chexbres died, the first thing that fed me . . ."

There may be passages scattered around in the literature of meals that describe with equal force the almost spiritual capacity of food, but none that reflects more clearly the changes that would take place in American restaurants, where the value of food went from something external ("poudingue inglesa" clearly Mazatlán 1941's stab at *le standing*) to something internal. The new ideal would become rusticity, not faux sophistication. It was a shift that would truly transform the American restaurant business. At first, it would liberate French and Italian restaurant owners in the United States from the straitjacket of gentility in which they'd always had to operate. But gradually it would affect the perception of other ethnic cuisines; whether Asian, Middle Eastern, or South American, as well as North American regional styles such as soul food, Tex-Mex, and southwestern. At its worst, this is our own age's version of continental cuisine, in which dishes with mahi mahi, miso, gnocchi, and Thai basil pesto have become as clichéd as steak Diane ever was (and a lot less wine-friendly). But at its best, it becomes truly innovative, a supranational style where culinary boundaries recede before the quality of restraint that all good food shares. This is a lot to lay at the feet of Mary Frances Kennedy Fisher enjoying a bowl of beans in Mazatlán in 1941. But it is important to note that in the year that Le Pavillon opened, the culinary sensibility that would grow to counter the supremacy of haute cuisine had already begun.

Such a transformation was a death knell to restaurants like Perino's. It is not enough to say that Perino's closed because fashions change. "Fashion" implies that, like lapel widths, it might return, and the economic conditions that made possible a seventeen-thousand-square-foot restaurant with chandeliers and scalloped booths that were yours for the night never will. What happened to Perino's was harsher, harder, and more final. Flamingo-pink was no longer glamorous but gaudy. A hovering maître d' didn't make diners feel powerful but uncomfortable. In short, the version of reality that Perino's offered no longer corresponded to that of enough potential customers. In fact, for many of them, it represented what Thorstein Veblen called in the 1899 study, *The Theory of the Leisure Class*, a prototype of "aesthetic nausea."

Veblen's analysis of the messages encrypted in fashion was brilliant. Not only was the expense of the item a means to demonstrate the wearer's wealth to others, but the slight impracticality of the well-dressed man or woman's wardrobe—the corset, the silk top hat, the white tie, the patent leather shoes—and the impossibility of performing physical work while wearing these articles was a means of signaling that the owners didn't even have to work in order to afford them.

Food is not without its own encrypted messages. Pierre Franey in his autobiography, *A Chef's Tale*, makes the subtle point that the reason why butter was used almost exclusively in haute cuisine was that using rendered fats such as lard or schmaltz were farmhouse methods of cooking and thus sent the opposite message to sophistication that haute cuisine was supposed to send. Similarly, the use of a menu written in French in a non-French-speaking country was a means by which a restaurant impressed its own elegance on customers who couldn't read it and flattered those who could. These principles did not change on a whim but through Veblen's "aesthetic nausea." This is what happens when the prevalent fashion no longer says what we want it to say about ourselves. When the dowager's daughter refuses to wear a corset, the gentleman's son to go out in spats. Culinarily, this is what happens when the customer is no longer impressed but instead disgusted by fish mousse in the shape of the Arc de Triomphe or when a *Michelin* two-star restaurant is allowed to use the fat rendered from the white fat that surrounds veal kidneys to do its pan cooking (as we used to do at Guy Savoy).

One rarely comes across the sort of review where the reviewer is stunningly aware of the aesthetic implications that are taking place in a particular restaurant. But one that was written by Caroline Bates in the October 1975 edition of *Gourmet* is just such a review. California, for *Gourmet*, had always been represented by the occasional story on the swallows of San Juan Capistrano or the shopping to be had in San Francisco's Union Square. But the editors realized that there might be more of interest going on in the most populous state in the Union, and in January 1974, they launched "Specialites de la Maison—California," a West Coast version of their New York review column that would be written by Caroline Bates.

The first restaurant she reviewed was Scandia, the fondly remembered Scandinavian establishment on Sunset Boulevard. Over the next year and a half, she weighed in on such disparate restaurants as René Verdon's Le Trianon (he had left the White House for San Francisco), Romeo Salta's original Chianti in Hollywood, and the Armenian-Russian restaurant Kavkaz, perched above the Sunset Strip. While the view from this restaurant did have a certain place-specific "smoggy charm"—and connoisseurs of Los Angeles macabre knew it to be the place where Sharon Tate and her friends enjoyed their last meal before returning to Cielo Drive—there was little about the restaurants reviewed in the column that made them indelibly Californian. They could just as easily have been reviewed in "Spécialités de la Maison—New York."

In the October 1975 issue she hit on a restaurant that couldn't. The cover shot of the magazine, a picture of the lobby of Claridge's Hotel in London, may have pointed to *Gourmet's* first love, European sophistication, but Bates's search for originality in California had led her to much more humble surroundings, a small restaurant in Berkeley called Chez Panisse.

"One evening some months ago, while diners in restaurants the length of California were facing that unholy trinity of onion soup, duckling à l'orange, and crème caramel, we were occupying a window table in the enclosed porch off the dining room at Chez Panisse and discovering a ramekin of mushrooms in the style of Quercy, roast duckling with fresh basil, and an almond tart surely made in heaven."

The review was enthusiastically positive. But perhaps most prescient of Bates was the way she spent more than a little time and space actually describing some of the people that were responsible for this restaurant. "Alice Waters, a onetime Montessori teacher, discovered France and French food at the age of nineteen. Upon her return home she cooked brilliant dinners for her friends, who encouraged her to start a restaurant. . . . Jeremiah Tower turned up fresh from the Harvard School of Architecture. Dining one evening at the restaurant, he admired a raspberry tart, criticized a soup, and subsequently became the principal chef."

There are many obvious differences between such a restaurant and Perino's. One was pink plaster, the other wood. One had a menu consisting of sixty entrées, the other a single fixed menu. At Perino's, the ideal ingredient was "flown-in" Dover sole, at Chez Panisse it would become "foraged" field greens. While the transformation in the culinary ideal as it was represented at Perino's and at Chez Panisse would be lasting and would include shifts in perception from "urbane" to "rustic" and—as per Fisher—food with an "outer" value to food with an "inner" value, the most telling difference between the restaurants may have been in the people who worked in them.

In a 1973 article about Perino's in the *Los Angeles Times* (as it began its long and ignominious slide toward a banquet-only formula, a move to downtown in 1980 to take advantage of the Olympics, and its final shuttering on Wilshire Boulevard in 1983), David Shaw described some of the cooks working in Perino's kitchen. Tito Loyo, the night fry cook, was seventy years old, of which thirty-nine had been spent at Perino's. Justino Suarez, the night pastry cook, was also seventy, of which twenty-three had been at this job. While such men had the experience to know how to keep a gallon of béarnaise from cur-dling over a three-hour service or how to deep-fry order after order of beautifully puffed *pommes soufflées*, they could not put the profes-sion of cooking within the larger context that the university-educated cooks at Chez Panisse could. For the cooks working behind the flamingo-pink walls at Perino's, cooking was a job. For those working behind the honeysuckle hedge at Chez Panisse, it was a solution.

◁═══▷

SLASH, BURN, FILET

On a stultifyingly hot August day in Berkeley, I walked up the stairs toward the Chez Panisse café to interview Alice Waters. At the top of the stairs, I was greeted by a manager who transmitted my name by telephone to someone else and then asked me to wait. I sat down at a table in the bar. It was two-thirty in the afternoon and there were still people enjoying lunch, sitting in the weak breeze that came in through the restaurant's windows. The cooks, all in the woven caps that across the country mark those having come out of the Chez Panisse style, were preparing for dinner. The posters of Marius and other characters from Marcel Pagnol's *Marseille Trilogy* hung over the stairwell. It was peaceful.

A few minutes later, Alice Waters appeared from a side door. She wore a lace dress and a straw bonnet that, though both were black, seemed comfortable in the heat. We shook hands and she graciously directed me toward a table by the open kitchen, where we sat down to talk. With a rapidity that made me think that this was the protocol for all interviews, a large bottle of sparkling water and two glasses were placed in front of us. I said something about how food had changed in California and she laughed and suggested I look at a Time-Life book of the late 1960s to see to what an extent this was so. Because I was having trouble visualizing Chez Panisse in its early days, I asked her to describe it and she helpfully did so. "Well, we used to have flowers in latte glasses on the tables," she started, clearly doing her best to remember. "I hired two French girls as waitresses because they wore short skirts and could give French attitude. Another waiter I hired because he arrived with, you know, one of those waiter's wallets and I thought he must know what he was doing. He eventually became a partner. . . . We started the single menu because that's the way you'd do it at home. I still don't know how to do à la carte."

We kept drinking the cool sparkling water in the sun-infused dining room and the happy re-creation of the past continued—together with several caveats that other people remembered the details better than she did. I would have come away from the interview as charmed by her unpretentious ways as many had been before me except for a very telling pause in the conversation. It came when I said "Who?" when she mentioned Mario Savio. There was a beat and it was as if in that split second she finally could place me as an interviewer and she understood that this interview was one of the most superficial kind. If I didn't know who Mario Savio was—and other than tell me he was part of the Berkeley Free Speech Movement of the 1960s she wasn't about to start explaining it—I would never really understand Chez Panisse.

I knew, as does anyone interested in the American restaurant business, that the entire California culinary movement had political beginnings. (Anyone who's heard one of its principals set the scene by saying, "In '72 they were still mining Haiphong Harbor," would be hard-pressed not to.) Having not experienced those times as an adult myself, I had tried to understand them through one of the period's seminal books, Herbert Marcuse's 1969 classic, *An Essay on Liberation*. Some of Marcuse's key concepts had struck me as strangely apt to the founding of a countercultural restaurant. Their cooperative nature was clearly a means of avoiding "the exploitative apparatus of business." Spending hours making a dish was a means of making "the process of production a process of creation." The very idea of working in a kitchen rather than toward the career one's degree had prepared one for was a means of participating in Marcuse's "great refusal."

But that was before I met Alice Waters and before I saw the look she gave me when I failed to recognize Mario Savio's name. I understood that this interpretation was not only superficial but also verged on being a caricature and if I hoped to understand Chez Panisse I was going to have to go deeper. Over the next several weeks, I spent time at the Central Library in San Francisco poring over the massive green tomes that comprise *The Readers' Guide to Periodical Literature* and the microfilmed archives of the *San Francisco Chronicle*. Two different things happened simultaneously. I did indeed find out more about Mario Savio and the politics of the 1960s, but as I did so, I became aware of my own biases. The moment these biases became clear to me was as I read a 1975 article in the *Chronicle* written by Ruth Stein and entitled "The Chefs of Berkeley—Educated and Well Fed." The article had the usual stuff about how pastry chef Lindsey Shere had a degree in French from UC Berkeley and even included a prototypical Berkeley quote from waiter Steve Crumley (masters' degree in linguistics): "There's a more relaxed attitude here. There aren't the pressures to be an aggressive achiever and settle the problems of the world. In Berkeley they just let people be." But the article changed tone, for me, at the quote from Alice Waters herself when she said of her staff of twenty-five: "Most every worker here is a displaced person from somewhere."

What had been an inchoate uneasiness with the philosophical underpinnings of the Berkeley style now rose to the surface at the sight of the word "displaced." That is not a word to be used lightly in the context of the restaurant business. Tito Loyo, from El Salvador, seventy years of age and still working as night fry cook at Perino's, may have felt displaced. Romeo Salta when he jumped ship in New York because he had no papers to land may have felt displaced. Henri Soulé when he cried on opening night of Le Pavillon because he had no family members with whom to share his joy may have felt displaced. Any newly arrived immigrant family that buys a few tables in a restaurant supply warehouse, cooks the food they know, have their children clean the beans at a table in the back, and send whichever relative speaks English best out to take the orders might—but probably won't—feel displaced. To read that white, middle-class, American-born, university graduates in a position to take advantage of every opportunity this country could offer felt displaced, sounded, at its most charitable, like a slight overstatement of the case.

But to understand how it had been meant I had to understand the times. According to the writer Leonard Michaels, that political tidal wave of the 1960s had begun in 1959, across the park from the library in which I now sat, on the steps and in the rotunda of the San Francisco City Hall. Here, the demonstrators that had gathered to protest the holding of meetings by the infamous House Committee on Un-American Activities were met by battalions of the San Francisco Police Department and in short order fire-hosed and dragged by the hair down the building's sweeping stairs. Within that context, one might well feel displaced.

Most of the demonstrators were students from either UC Berkeley or San Francisco State and the scene could indeed be considered the opening spark of the student movement of the next decade. Soon that fire had been fueled by civil rights activism and the growing disaffection of many of the Berkeley students for the increasingly impersonal university experience—the "multiversity"—as envisioned by the president of the University of California system, Clark Kerr. (Kerr was unfairly demonized by the student movement. He himself was formed by an earlier era of agitation and was co-author of a report entitled *Documentary History of the Strike of the Cotton Pickers in California in 1933* that state librarian Kevin Starr has called "a masterpiece of Depression documentary art.") With the founding in Berkeley of the Free Speech Movement in October 1964, the two fronts of the fire—student and civil rights activism—joined. The movement's defining moment was when Mario Savio, a twenty-two-year-old mathematics student and a graduate of Martin Van Buren High School in the Bronx—who had spent the previous summer, the "Freedom Summer," working in Mississippi for the Student Nonviolent Coordinating Committee (SNCC)—gave an impassioned speech while standing on top of a campus Police Department car. The car's progress was being impeded (and would be for thirty-two hours) by students who were themselves trained in the nonviolent techniques of CORE (Congress of Racial Equality). Inside the car was a certain Jacob Weinberg, who had just been arrested for handing out civil rights literature on campus, an activity that the UC regents—even as they gave an honorary degree to the Shah of Iran and maintained research facilities at the Lawrence Radiation Laboratory in Livermore, which were critically important in the building of nuclear weapons—believed to be overly political. Within this context also, one might feel displaced.

In 1965, the *New York Times Magazine* published a cover article, "The Berkeley Affair." The author, A. M. Raskin, an assistant editor of the editorial page, described how Savio, instantly recognizable by the fleece-lined coat that he always wore, almost refused to participate in the interview for fear it would perpetuate the personality cult, which he feared. Jacob Weinberg had gone on to civil rights activism with CORE and was not available. It was the movement's press officer who allowed that there were "strains" within the movement regarding how to proceed, and that one thought under consideration was to establish, not far from campus, a cooperative type of coffeehouse. "It would be a civilized gathering place in the best European manner," he said, "a suitable forum for debate and discussion."

Raskin, a veteran of the student movement at CCNY (City College of New York) in the 1930s, clearly thought that "setting up an espresso joint as a monument to their mutiny" was somewhat lightweight. He did, however, admit that these students were a "tougher, smarter breed" than his own generation, which had "chickened out" of picketing their own commencement for fear of losing their degrees.

The coffeehouse idea was, in fact, an early formulation of what would eventually happen. By 1966, the organizational skills that had come out of the Free Speech Movement (and one of its offshoots, the Vietnam Day Committee) coalesced around Robert Scheer's campaign for California's Seventh Congressional District, which at the time encompassed both the Berkeley campus and the Oakland ghetto. For his supporters, it was a disastrous election. Not only did Scheer lose in the primary, but in the governor's race, two-time governor Pat Brown lost in a landslide to Ronald Reagan. It was in this atmosphere of lost illusions that Alice Waters, a veteran of the Free Speech Movement and Scheer's campaign manager in Berkeley, moved toward the idea of creating her own reality.

Eventually, she would reprise the press officer's idea for a coffeehouse in the best European manner that would be near campus, except she would up the ante and start a restaurant. The culinary vision that it would be based on was nothing less than that of the small, friendly, good, French country restaurant, that of the idyllic France; not unlike that which Fernand Point had perfected, Henri Soulé venerated, and Joseph Wechsberg lauded. That none of the people attempting this feat had ever actually worked in a restaurant did not, in the spirit of the times, seem to present an obstacle.

The name "Chez Panisse" is indicative of how the restaurant was created out of the conditions of the times. It is not Chez Jean, Chez Gaston, Chez any French person who ever opened a restaurant. It is instead named after a character in Marcel Pagnol's 1933 *Marseille Trilogy* that Alice Waters saw, as part of a Pagnol cycle, in the art house Surf Theater in San Francisco's fogbound Sunset District in early 1971.

The setting of the trilogy is the Vieux Port of Marseille. Here, the men spend their days sitting around César's Bar de la Marine as the women cry out the price of the *coquillages* that they sell. Life is one long wait for the next delivery of Picon until César's son, Marius, falls for Fanny, a daughter of Honorine, one of the cockle-sellers. In addition to Fanny, Marius also has a yearning for the large sailboats that go in and out of the port and finally, torn between his two loves, he chooses the life of a sailor and takes to sea on a long voyage—but not before leaving Fanny pregnant.

At this, Panisse, the local sailmaker and an old friend of César's—who has always had a thing for Fanny—asks her to marry him promising that he will raise the child, Césariot, as if it were his own. Unhappily at first, she does. Over the course of the trilogy, all the expected plot points occur: Marius eventually returns, is rejected by Fanny, who chooses loyal Panisse, Césariot grows up to discover that Panisse is not his father, and Panisse becomes deathly ill. The local doctor, thinking that the priest is moving too fast in arriving at the house to administer the last rites, tells him, "If you want to use your oils so badly go and make an aïoli!" But neither one of them can save Panisse. After he dies, César sets about reuniting Fanny and Marius with the blessing of Césariot.

To have seen this cycle in France at the time it came out was probably to appreciate at face value the many twists of the melodramatic plot. To have seen it in France in 1971, it would probably be impossible not to superimpose a nostalgic element into it for a way of life that had disappeared forever. To have seen it in San Francisco in 1971 would lead to a totally different interpretation. Here, among the intrigues of the characters, was a Provençal version of many of the values of the counterculture. Camaraderie, community, human warmth, and, increasingly, aïoli. For Alice Waters, a Montessori teacher from northern New Jersey who'd lived as a student in France and was about to open a small Berkeley restaurant, it was enough of an inspiration to open it under the spiritual guidance, so to speak, of old Panisse.

If Pagnol set the scene at Chez Panisse, the food writer Elizabeth David set the table. David was born in England in 1913, but it was a year spent in the Paris suburb of Passy at age sixteen that forever marked her with the pleasures of the bourgeois table. During the late 1930s, she lived in Greece and Italy. During the war, she married an English officer in the Indian Army with whom she lived in Egypt and briefly in India. Her marriage would not last long and she returned to England in 1946. Her travels in the Mediterranean, however, gave her the subject of her first book, *A Book of Mediterranean Food*, which appeared in 1950. The author photograph, a moody chiaroscuro credited to "Hassia, Cairo," showed she knew whereof she spoke. Some of the descriptions showed the length she would always go to in the interest of authenticity (who, indeed, who has ever been to Greece could forget "the sound of air gruesomely whistling through sheep's lungs frying in oil"?). But it was the frontispiece of the book that gave an immediate image of what the author was trying to communicate. Before the recipes for *brandade de morue*, Greek avgolemono, and Provençal anchoïade; before all the long quotes from Henry James, D. H. Lawrence, Tobias Smollett (David's way of providing context), there was a simple line drawing by John Minton of a Mediterranean port—for all the world the Vieux Port—and a beautiful young cockleseller and a handsome young sailor toasting with glasses of wine. They could easily have been Marius and Fanny. From the vantage of

Berkeley, it was as if the aesthetic of Pagnol had found its method-ology.

David's ideal eating place would never be the grand Parisian restaurant. Occasionally, a *Michelin* two-star like Madame Baraterro's Hôtel du Midi in Lamastre, where she stayed on demipension rates, won her praise. But she would always feel most at home in the small, bustling restaurants of Europe, the quayside cafés, the bistros, the trattorias, the *routiers*, those noisy, lively restaurants where French truck drivers ate. "Good cooking is honest, sincere and simple," she wrote, positing her culinary philosophy against "the absurd lengths of the complicated and so called Haute Cuisine." Reading that chicken and fish veloutés and lobster butter "belonged rather to the methods of restaurant cooking and professional chefs than to country and household meals" was surely reassuring to the university graduates who cooked at Chez Panisse and who, at first, could make neither a chicken or fish velouté or a lobster butter. But to the cooks at Chez Panisse in 1971 (a year before "they were still mining Haiphong Harbor"), what was more important than David's technical principles was the sheer transporting power of her prose. You read it and it took you away.

A Book of Mediterranean Food opens with a passage that has the cadence of a culinary Churchill: "From Gibraltar to the Bosphorus, down the Rhone Valley, through the great seaports of Marseilles, Barcelona and Genoa, across to Tunis and Alexandria, embracing all the Mediterranean islands, Corsica, Sardinia, Crete, the Cyclades . . . The ever recurring elements in the food throughout these countries are the oil, the saffron, the garlic, the pungent local wines, the aromatic perfume of rosemary, wild marjoram and basil drying in the kitchens, the brilliance of the market stalls piled high with pimentos, aubergines, tomatoes, olives, melons, figs and limes, the great heaps of shiny fish, silver, vermilion or tiger-striped, and those long needle

fish whose bones mysteriously turn green when they are cooked."
There yet?

Her second book, *French Country Cooking* (1951), does not slack off. "France's culinary reputation.. . . is best appreciated at the river-side inns, in unknown cafés along the banks of the Burgundy canal, patronized by men who sail the great petrol and timber barges to and from Marseille, great eaters and drinkers most of them, in the hos-pitable farmhouses of the Loire and the Dordogne, of Normandy and the Correze, in sea-port bistros frequented by fishermen, sailors, ship chandlers . . ."

Her third book, *Italian Food* (1954), kept up the pace. "Of all the spectacular food markets in Italy the one near the Rialto in Venice must be the most remarkable. The light of the Venetian dawn in early summer—you must be about at four o'clock in the morning to see the market coming to life—is so limpid and so still that it makes every separate vegetable and fruit and fish luminous with a life of its own, with unnaturally heightened colors and clear stenciled outlines. Here the cabbages are cobalt blue, the beetroots deep rose, the lettuces clear pure green, sharp as glass. Bunches of gaudy gold marrow flowers show off the elegance of pink-and-white marbled bean pods, prim-rose potatoes, green plums, green peas. The color of the peaches, cherries and apricots, packed in boxes lined with blue paper matching the blue canvas trousers worn by the men unloading the gondolas, are reflected in the rose-red mullet and the orange vongole and cannestrelle, which have been pried out of their shells and heaped in baskets."

This has the specificity of an actor's exercise, the realness of a scene one could as easily walk into as turn the page. One can only really paint such a vivid picture from a distance. David was writing this not looking out at anything resembling her subject but in a Lon-don that was still under the constraints of food rationing and very much carried the scars of war. Many parts of the city had not changed much from the description Muriel Spark gives of London in the opening of her novel *The Girls of Slender Means*. A city where the streets "were lined with buildings in bad repair or in no repair at all, bombsites piled high with stony rubble, houses like giant teeth in which decay had been drilled out, leaving only the cavity. Some bomb-ripped buildings looked like the ruins of ancient castles until, at a closer view, the wallpapers of various quite normal rooms would be visible, room above room, exposed, as on a stage, with one wall missing; a fourth or fifth floor ceiling, most of all the staircases survived, like a new art form, leading up and up to an unspecified destination that made unusual demands on the mind's eye."

In this landscape, to write about Levantine fishing ports one has known, the eating habits of Burgundian bargemen, or the color of freshly landed fish in Italian markets is a form of escape. In the introduction to *A Book of Mediterranean Food*, she made clear that this was her intention. "I hope to give some idea of the lovely cookery of those regions to people who do not already know them," she wrote, typically using a minor key, "and to stir the memories of those who have eaten this food on its native shores, and who would like sometimes to bring a flavor of those blessed lands of sun and sea and olive trees into their English kitchens."

I got to see David's magical ability to transport her readers early on in my life. When my parents divorced, my mother took my sister, Micaela, and me out of Spain, where we'd grown up, and back to Ireland, where she'd grown up and from where she'd escaped at the age of eighteen. We lived in a garret of a building on a Georgian square in central Dublin. Needing money and knowing how to cook, she had a résumé typed up and dropped copies off in domestic agencies and restaurants. In the résumé, she wrote that she'd "lived and kept house" in Switzerland, France, and Spain. It was a phrase, I now realize, straight out of Elizabeth David's bio in the Penguin edition of her books where she is described as having "lived and kept house in

France, Italy, Greece, Egypt and India." Soon my mother had a succession of kitchen jobs—places where during holidays I would learn how to pick blanched sweetbreads, clean leeks by slicing them almost their entire length to loosen their leaves and then dunk in and out of full sinks of water to shake out any earth, where I was handed a worn-down paring knife and shown how to scrape off the beards in sacks of mussels. On Saturdays, I'd come home from boarding school and I'd hear my mother come in from the lunchtime shift, open a can of beer and lie down on her bed for a few minutes. The books she kept beside her bed were the Penguin editions of Elizabeth David. I now realize that as my sister and I were filled with all the new smells and tastes of food we'd never known in Spain—that of salt butter, milky tea, soda scones, sizzling rashers—she kept dipping in and out of her collection of Elizabeth David, not because she needed a recipe for that night but because the recipes reminded her of tastes and smells she had known: of olive oil and garlic and the precise color of landed fish in any one of many Mediterranean ports she'd sat at, of places where she'd been happy, places where she'd "kept house."

Like M. F. K. Fisher eating her beans in Mazatlán Airport, like Elizabeth David starting to write about the Mediterranean in the bitterly cold English winter of 1947, like my mother, forty, divorced, with two children, reading in a garret in a country from which she'd once fled, so Alice Waters in 1966, in the year that Robert Scheer lost in the congressional primary and Ronald Reagan became governor of California, found that her world—the world she wished for, certainly—had been destroyed and decided to put it back together through food.

TOWARD
CALIFORNIA CUISINE

For a time, before he bought a van with bad brakes, Jeremiah Tower would read Elizabeth David on a bus crossing the Bay Bridge. When he'd been handed the Chez Panisse kitchen's well-worn copies of David's books, he was simply told, "Cook this." With that gesture, he knew he'd become chef. Because no one on the crew was a professionally trained chef, cookbooks were of extraordinary importance. Once they found one that spoke to them, they didn't just read it, they drained it to its lees. For Tower, the process was simple: read about pipérade on the way to work because pipérade was on that night's menu. Read how the Greeks roasted a whole lamb, because that's what someone was bringing down from Dal Porto Ranch. Soon Waters and Tower had found an author whose style captivated them as much as David's in Richard Olney, an American living in France since the 1950s.

Olney had initially moved to France to paint. The value of the dollar at the time had allowed him to also experience dishes such as *poularde à la vapeur de Lucien Tendret* (a truffled Bresse chicken cooked in the steam of a double consommé) at Alexandre Dumaine's legendary Hôtel de la Côte-d'Or in Burgundy. He was hooked. In time, he was cooking pot-au-feu in his Paris garret, contributing to the magazine *Cuisine et Vins de France* (the only American to ever do so) and eventually writing his first two seminal cookbooks, *The French Menu Cookbook* (1970) and *Simple French Food* (1974).

Olney understood the emotional dimension that certain foods had for the French and he was brilliantly able to communicate it. Thus, in *Simple French Food*, he described braised meats as representing "the philosophical cornerstone of French family cooking; they embody—or spark—something akin to an ancestral or racial memory of farmhouse kitchens—of rustic tables laid by mothers, grandmothers, or old retainers." In hindsight, one reads such passages with a certain nostalgia because they evoke an idea of a France that—during the very same period that the books were being published—was quickly disappearing. The haute cuisine bourgeoise restaurant tradition that allowed for slow-cooked dishes such as a truffled chicken steamed in the vapor of a consommé was giving way to the decrees of nouvelle cuisine. The *routes nationales* along whose borders so many great restaurants had thrived (Hôtel de la Côte-d'Or, Hostellerie de la Poste in Avallon, and La Pyramide, to name but a few) were giving way to the six-lane *autoroutes*. Furthermore, the era of the ocean liner, the very symbol of European travel to Americans, was coming to an end. In 1974, Olney booked passage on the last westbound voyage of the *France*. He was traveling to the United States to promote *Simple French Food*, a book that conjured up a France that was swiftly disappearing. Little did he know he was about to meet a group of people who were determined to re-create it.

He was signing books in the Williams-Sonoma store in San

Francisco early in 1975 when Alice Waters and Jeremiah Tower walked up to him. An exchange of pleasantries led to an invitation from Waters that he join them at Chez Panisse that evening with someone she knew to be a friend from his Paris days in the early 1950s, the film-maker Kenneth Anger. Thus, with an ability to fuse disciplines that was somewhat typical of Chez Panisse, the *auteur* of the underground cult classic *Scorpio Rising* enjoyed a meal that reflected the glories of provincial France with the author of two books that would eventually play an important role in transforming the American culinary lexicon.

Simple French Food was perhaps the more influential of the two books. It contains an important section on "thoughts about improvisation" and its recipes are less classical and communicate a more coherent culinary vision. *The French Menu Cookbook*, however, because it was published first and marks the original formulation of Olney's philosophy, is a better prism through which to study the influence he had on the Chez Panisse style. The most notable aspect of this influence—unexpected in an author and a restaurant devoted to capturing the essence of France—would be the transferal of the restaurant's source of culinary inspiration from France to California.

The cover of the book is deceptively unoriginal. Its colors are red, white, and blue, with the book's subtitle framed within a gilded border ("The food and wine of France—Season by delicious Season—in beautifully composed menus for American dining and entertaining by an American living in Paris and Provence"). This, as the publisher, Simon & Schuster, clearly went to the trouble of pointing out, was a known entity: a French cookbook written for Americans by an American.

Once inside the cover, however, the reader found Olney admitting in the preface that "the book is essentially a personal gastronomic manifesto." Many aspects of the manifesto corresponded to the fundamental beliefs of Chez Panisse. It championed the essential simplicity that Chez Panisse always strove for ("A perfect meal can be many things," Olney wrote, "a plate of lentils with a boiled sausage, a green salad, a piece of cheese and a bottle of young Beaujolais"). It insisted on going upstream from the finished meal to the agricultural principles that produced it, describing how "the excitement of eating a freshly picked fruit or vegetable at the peak of its seasonal richness is forever deadened by the dull and listless year-round absorption of its shadow."

In hindsight, one can also see clear practical influences that the book had on the Chez Panisse style: Olney gave a diagram of his home's open grill, and grilling became the restaurant's cooking technique of choice. Olney gave the Paris address from which could be ordered seeds for little-known field salads such as roquette, mâche, pissenlit, and mesclun, and they quickly became indispensable building blocks of the restaurant's salads.

The greatest influence was not practical but philosophical and involved two different aspects of menu writing. The first was the principle of always using simple language: "Classical appellations have not been tampered with," Olney wrote in the preface, "(it would be a pity to deprive Melba of her peaches and ice cream), but, when possible, I have stuck to simple, descriptive titles and have avoided the fanciful." The second was his call for seeing the actual writing of a menu, with the "juxtaposition of cold and hot, crisp and creamy, rough and smooth, sauced and dry," as an opportunity to create what he called "a gastronomic aesthetic."

Two aspects of Tower's menus are of particular interest in this regard. The first is the development toward a style; the second is the gradual discovery of California as a source of culinary inspiration. Tower's early menus seem blinded by their themes; they read less like interpretative exercises and more like stylistic stunts. In the summer of 1975, the first course of "Eliza Acton's English Dinner," which commemorated Waterloo, was "Salmon cooked in white wine, pounded with butter, then preserved in ramekins." (Was one meant to eat it or unearth it?) Three months later, during the weeklong series of Dalíesque "Dinners for Gala," the offerings were strictly surreal: "A salad not composed by Alexandre Dumas of beets, celery-root, potatoes, lettuce and Maxim's sauce." But by March 1976, Tower had reached a very French moment in his career. One that for a French chef is an inescapable stage in the discovery of an individual cooking style, and that is to show his mastery of the recipes in the one book he's carried with him since the *école hôtelière* where he began his studies, Escoffier's *Le Guide Culinaire*.

Typically for Chez Panisse, the exercise was framed in intellectual terms. "The last three weeks in March," read the program that was printed up for the occasion, "will celebrate a great master, a great pupil and their followers. First, a week of Escoffier, who introduced the 20th Century to great French cooking and vice-versa; followed by two weeks of menus devised for Chez Panisse by Richard Olney, who renewed the passion and updated it. If the price for a particular dinner sometimes seems a bit stiff for the apparent humbleness of the ingredients, it is because of the immense care and labor involved. Following these three weeks, we will experiment with an à la carte grill-type menu and concept, emerging from Escoffier's innovations, so that the public may evaluate the two distinct styles."

The tone communicates the passion with which the exercise was undertaken—but it was not a passion that was easy to communicate to the greater public. The first dish got howls of derision from the *San Francisco Chronicle*'s master of three-dot journalism, Herb Caen: "Chez Panisse is doing a week of recipes from the immortal Chef Auguste Escoffier's Guide Culinaire (1902). The very first item on Panisse's menu being 'crêpe with sterlet caviar from Sacramento' . . . Sacramento? Vassyou dere. Owgoost." The use of a California place-name within the context of a French meal may have been original enough to make it into Caen's daily column, but it was also indicative of something that had been happening on a parallel track to the development of an actual cooking style (from Escoffier to Olney to grilling in this particular exercise) and that was the discovery of California as a place from which culinary inspiration could be drawn. If, simply put, that meant making a connection between what was grown and what was eaten, no enterprise would seem more doomed to fail.

Pull off Interstate 5 just north of Stockton, close to the meeting point of the Sacramento and San Joaquin Rivers and the only place to eat for miles around will be Rockie's truck stop. Here, the truckers sit at booths with phones where they can use their phone cards; the waitresses call you "Hon" and have perfected a way of bantering with the truckers while they pour endless cups of coffee. It is indeed a cheerful place and the steak and eggs are hearty, but to sit in a booth at Rockie's, and to look out at the flat asparagus fields that surround the restaurant knowing that there isn't a chance you will be offered asparagus in any form, is to understand something about California, and that is that food here is devoid of any context, and for all the power of California agriculture, it has no relationship to food.

California was never homesteaded but deeded in great swaths to the railway companies and the wealthy, irrigated not by rain but by huge tax-funded projects, and the enterprise of growing crops there had never had much of a pastoral quality. What historical context California food did have was often better ignored; the result was that there was no connection at all between what was grown and what was eaten. Sheila Hibben's 1946 classic *American Regional Food* is a good example. In a country of "Jambalaya Lafite" and "Cowpuncher Beans"; a country where the culinary regionalism produced such evocative dishes as Connecticut's "Hartford Election Cake" (in whose name one can almost smell the celebratory whiskey on the ward bosses' breath), Tennessee's "Murray County Corn Meal Dodgers for Potlickers" (whose name conjures up the washed-out housecoats of the women who made them), or Pennsylvania's "Short Ribs of Beef with Sauerkraut and Ferino Dumplings" (can one not almost hear the Germanically inflected English spoken around this table?); into this earthy, vital mix, California sashays with its handful of recipes like some vapid, oversunned bimbo. With the sole exception of "Hangtown Fry," the state's offerings are singularly dull. From the "Tuna Fish Casserole"—the key ingredient of which is a seven-ounce can of tuna—to the grape salads and avocado spreads, the recipes might as well come from the most simplistic California Department of Agriculture leaflet.

If the food of California had a connection to its agriculture that went deeper than this, it would have been inspired by the food of Asia. The Chinese built the transcontinental railway that, with its completion in 1869, created a rapid transportation method for shipments east. This allowed crops such as citrus and perishable vegetables to supplant wheat and later sugar beets as the state's main crops. The completion of that same railway system simultaneously created a suddenly unemployed labor force to grow and pack the produce that it was now profitable to grow. After the Chinese, generations of Filipino, Japanese, and Mexican farm workers helped reclaim the wetlands and valleys and turn them into some of the country's richest land.

But drive west from Rockie's, across the flat delta roads to "Chinese" towns such as Isleton and Walnut Grove, whose founders built the levees of the Sacramento that made fruit farming in this area possible, and you'll see that the Chinese writing under the town's laundry is faded, the clapboards of the local Chinese card club are loose; you might hear the happy, tuba-driven rhythm of a Mexican *banda* number come through an open window, but you'll know that the Chinese force that made possible all the miles of surrounding orchards is spent.

Drive north along the curving banks of the Sacramento and you can stop in the shadow of the state capitol, at Eighth and L Streets, at Frank Fat's, the restaurant that's been known for decades as the place where all political matters could be settled over generous portions of Chinese food. Frank Fat is no longer there to beat a path to a table for one of many governors of the state, but still you will enjoy the atmosphere. (The old men discreetly shooting dice at the bar, the look on the face of the newly elected representative from some valley town, come in with a party fixer for the requisite first slice of banana cream pie, who nervously shakes the hand of Frank Fat's son Wing Fat and in general wears a suit with a lack of ease that must have been reassuring to the voters of his district.) You will enjoy the food: the hot and sour soup ladled by the waiter, the simple stir-fries, yes, even the banana cream pie. But maybe in the fact that Frank Fat's is so Americanized that they don't even offer chopsticks, you might see that Chinese food has always adapted itself to its environment. In Havana, it led to the Cuban-Chinese diner; in Sacramento, it wasn't about to try to make a connection between produce and food.

Catty-corner from Frank Fat's is the Sacramento Greyhound station. Here, in the winter dusk, as they stand around waiting for buses to Stockton or Reno, one sees a certain kind of American that in larger cities one is unused to seeing. The new windbreakers, the no-known-brand sneakers, the thin, blond, always washed and invariably swept-back hair that is the pride of either sex and marks them as descendants of the families who escaped the Oklahoma dust bowl in the Depression and came in caravans of beat-up cars to California. Like the Chinese, Japanese, Filipino, and Mexican workers, they, too, played a huge role in the development of the state's agriculture and like them they also failed to make a connection between what they grew and what they ate.

The derogatory name "Okie," which they were soon given, is indicative of how they were treated. Faced with common landowner practices such as overadvertising for workers at harvesttime so that the unnecessarily large number of workers that showed up would drive down the daily wage, they organized and paid for it in blood.

The labor history of California agriculture as told in Carey McWilliams's 1939 *Factories in the Fields* is a story of uprisings and bloody suppressions. During the 1936 Salinas lettuce packers' strike, the lettuce producers placed machine-gun posts on the roofs of their packinghouses while bands of vigilantes armed with ax handles roamed the town's streets. The scene during the 1933 cotton pickers' strike was so tense that a reporter from the *Los Angeles Times* could write about it only as if writing a wartime dispatch: "The Tulare County Fairgrounds have been turned into a stockade," he wrote, "and the police are rounding up strikers and rioters and putting them in the stockade incommunicado. King's County is an armed camp."

These were the means used to maintain the national image of California agriculture as an idyllic place of bougainvillea-covered ranchos where pretty girls smiled up from the side panels of orange crates. The orange, in fact, became the symbol of the state's agricultural concerns. For a 1964 promotional event called "California Comes to New York," the lobby of the Waldorf was lined with flown-in orange trees. The governor and his wife hosted the invited luminaries. (James Beard enjoyed the California dates, which, when pitted, rolled in bacon and brown sugar and broiled, were the perfect hors d'oeuvre for the period, and he enjoyed the use that artichoke hearts were put to in fondue.) But the detail that grabs one's attention today is not the many possible uses of California produce but the atmospherics required for its promotion. The governor and his wife, the lobby of the Waldorf filled with flown-in orange trees—it reads like some multinational launching a product. One could be forgiven for thinking California wasn't a state at all but an agricultural conglomerate.

Cesar Chavez and the grape strike that the United Farm Workers organized against some of the state's biggest grape growers would eventually give a better picture of what was going on in the fields of California. It began in the town of Delano in Kern County in

1965 and soon snowballed into a powerful labor movement. With coverage in the national press, the source of California agriculture was no longer seen as an idyllic, indeterminate spot but, as in Steinbeck's time, a very real place of grim migrant labor camps.

The vagueness with which the actual site of California agriculture was thought of had always been one of the major impediments for the popularization of California wines. The very name "tank car wine," which was often given to it after the transportation method in which it was shipped east, is indicative of the way in which it was regarded. Unlike many other crops of California's bounty, grape-growing and wine-making had never been reflected in the state's sun-kissed image. Yes, people knew wine came from California, but that was almost like saying it came from somewhere west of the Rockies. In wine terms, it had no *terroir*.

This placeless sense becomes quite clear when one sees that the place it did often try to associate itself with was not California at all but France. A half-page in Sherry's 1964 catalogue promotes St. Michel Mountain Rouge as "The Cheerful 'Vin du Pays' of California." Should that not prove enough of an incentive for the potential buyer, a secondary reason for purchasing the wine was given in an Aaronian bit of number-crunching: "5 bottles @ $1.30 each of cheapest good California wine costs $6.50. Equal quantity of St. Michel in gallon jug costs $2.79. Saving you per gallon $3.71." This is putting the best possible light on jug wine but, absent all the usual promotional tools of the trade (appeals to class, sophistication, foreign lands, and humor), there was very little else for the natural-born salesman to go on.

California wine would gradually shift from being about jug wines to being about grape varietals. (Today, the victory of varietals is so complete that even jug wines are labeled under their grape type and, sick of reading about the "spicy fruit" that invariably describes the "bouquet" in these reds, one finds oneself reaching for such blended stalwarts as Gallo's Hearty Burgundy because it at least can recapture the walk-up or semester in which one drank it first.) There are several reasons for this transformation. None, of course, is greater than the sheer technical abilities of the people making the wines. The generation of André Tchelistcheff, the legendary winemaker at Beaulieu, Louis Martini, and Martin Ray would be reinforced by Robert Mondavi, Warren Winiarski, Joe Heitz, Paul Draper, Bernard Portet, Miljenko "Mike" Grgich, Joseph Phelps, and many others; who were themselves followed by a younger generation, including, tellingly, the younger Gallos. With these men and women, the perception of California wines had finally shifted from the jug to the magnum, from the tank car to the French oak barrel.

This perception of "new California" wines is well illustrated by the graphic techniques used in the labels. Gone are the high-gloss, gilded scrolls that jug wines had often used to improve their image. The new labels, woodcut, matte, increasingly deckle-edged, communicated an understated confidence to the wineries that was similar to some of the best in France. Malette Dean's design for the Mondavi label, showing the winery set against the Mayacamas Mountains that separate the valleys of Napa and Sonoma, has all the sense of place of the discreetly sized Château Lafite-Rothschild label which shows the château nestled in a copse of trees and which, in its engraved simplicity, communicates all the pastoral calm of a summer day in the Médoc. Similarly, the single stag of the Stag's Leap label has all the iconic simplicity of the tower on Château Latour's, while Ridge Vineyards' utilitarian, almost industrial typeface gives a visual cohesion to their many different wines that is similar in effect to the instantly recognizable labels of the Domaine de la Romanée-Conti.

While the technical abilities of the wine-makers was an important factor in the qualitative change of California wines and the visual design of labels reflected a shift in perception, the actual sense of California as a place from which good wines could come was first and foremost a semantic concern, one that Frank Schoonmaker had addressed as early as 1941 in *American Wines*, the book he co-authored with Tom Marvel. "Already, intelligent wine drinkers all over the country are asking why honest, American place names and grape variety names cannot be used for honest, American wines. To these persons (and there are more of them everyday) Lake Erie Island Catawba has a better ring than 'Grand Duke Rhine Wine'; Napa Valley Zinfandel than 'Royal Charter Brand Claret'; Livermore Valley Sauvignon than 'Golden Glow Haut Sauterne' and Lake Canandaigua Elvira than 'Private Stock Moselle.'"

Clearly, in wine, specificity meant quality and a shift away from brand-names to place-names was a prerequisite for a sense of *terroir* to be possible in California. But there is another function that putting place-names on a label performs and that, simply put, is it gives the drinking of that wine an emotional dimension. To each his own bank of images, but mention St. Romain to me and I see the tiny village high in the hills of the Côte de Beaune and I hear the pounding mallets of the coopers at François Frères reverberating all the way down the valley road. Say Appellation Pauillac Controlée and I remember one blisteringly hot day in Pauillac and drinking a *citron pressé* in the shaded terrace of one of the rundown cafés that face the Gironde. While France and Italy had always had it, California had to invent it. As the perception of where California wines came from changed from the vast central valley tract to the microclimate, the language the labels used to reflect it came to be a highly specific one of ridges, ranches, lanes, coasts, hills, and creeks. This not only communicated the uniqueness of a vineyard but also, more subtly, the very European idea of the poetry of a place.

The French had always understood the need for a certain poetic license when it came to naming dishes. Coq au Chambertin is not actually made with costly Chambertin (at least not when a French chef makes it), but it sounds grander than coq au vin. Similarly, a sauce made from the white wine and fish stock in which some fillets of sole have been poached—with the addition of mushrooms, shallots, and, at the end, butter and parsley—is made all the more appetizing by being given the heartwarming name *bonne femme*, or "good woman."

The menus of Chez Panisse reached this poetic stage paradoxically by reversing what the French had always done. Instead of calling a dish by a pretty name, they called it by its ingredients. Thus, at Chez Panisse, *brandade de morue* became "Specialty of Provence—salt cod creamed with garlic and olive oil, served with croutons fried in olive oil." The classic *billi-bi* was "Soup of mussel broth lightly thickened with egg yolks and cream." Even the humble *œufs en gelée* became "Eggs poached and served in a gelee with fresh tarragon." This was not only following Olney's call for simplicity of language but, as with Schoonmaker's point about the naming of wine, was also meant to counter the equation, all too familiar to American diners, that the grander the name of the dish the worse it was likely to be.

While this poetic specificity did indeed communicate quality, it did not communicate a sense of place. Not the way the French had mastered it, where a dish that used the wine of a region could actually define the region. *Poulet au vin jaune is* the Jura region. A *matelote* of lamprey eels in a red wine sauce *is* Saint-Émilion. The *jambon à la Chablesienne* that my grandparents ate at the Hostellerie de la Poste in Avallon on July 10, 1956 (when one was celebrating the end of thirty years at Ludwig Baumann note was made of such things) defines Chablis. California too would reach this stage where the food and wine joined to define a region and the Zinfandel grape would be the means to make the connection.

The grape itself was one with an indigenous authenticity. Unlike Pinot Noir, which was kept out of the famous 1976 blind tasting in Paris (which legitimized the entire industry when certain California Cabernets and Chardonnays received higher scores than their French counterparts) because it could not compete against great Burgundies, Zinfandel could not be entered because there were no French wines for it to compete against. There was something *hors-concours* about Zinfandel. While it grew in Napa, Sonoma, Santa Clara, and Mendocino counties, it was the Zinfandel that grew in the untrellised vineyards of the Sierra foothills in Amador County that came to reflect the culinary style that was being developed in the kitchen of Chez Panisse.

Not only could it be drunk young, a factor that during the yearly celebration for the arrival of Zinfandel Nouveau gave it the requisite French angle (finally, a true Californian *vin du pays*), but it was very adaptable to food. A Chez Panisse recipe such as Amador County lamb with spring garlic and Amador County Zinfandel sauce captured this perfectly. Here, as in France, the wine of a certain region was being used in a dish that defined that region. Here was an unexpected twist: the language was English but the message was French. Amador County, and by extension Berkeley, Northern California, and indeed the entire state was a gastronomic region.

Because this core principle, once it had been force-fed through the American promotional machine, came out being called "California Cuisine"; and because it was a style that swept across the country, it is often described as having been arrived at not gradually but in a moment of enlightenment. That moment came as a result of the need at Chez Panisse for a different daily menu. Tower had done dinners from the books of Elizabeth David and Richard Olney. He had done theme dinners like the Escoffier series and a Sauternes dinner and dinners inspired by the French regions. By the late summer of 1976, he had worked his way through the obvious choices of Provence, Normandy, Brittany, Alsace, Gascony, and the Basque country and was starting to think in terms of having to do a less-inspiring region such as Corsica. That's when his broad reading led him to Charles Ranhofer's *A Selection of Interesting Bills of Fare of Delmonico's from 1862 to 1894.* It is a massive tome. But leafing through it, he stopped dead in his tracks at a recipe in the chapter on soups. "Cream of Green Corn à la Mendocino" the recipe read. Mendocino! Not the small town up the Northern California coast that most everyone in Berkeley knew for the quality and quantity of the marijuana it produced? The very one. To think that Ranhofer, the chef at Delmonico's, had heard of the place was amazing enough. To see it written within the syntax of a French recipe was revelatory. The switch had been thrown. California could be approached as one would a French region.

Soon the menu had been written. On October 17, 1976, it was presented. It was called the "Northern California Regional Dinner." The price was $20.

Spenger's Tomales Bay bluepoint oysters on ice
Cream of fresh corn soup, Mendocino style, with crayfish butter
Big Sur Garrapata Creek smoked trout steamed over California bay leaves
Monterey Bay prawns sautéed with garlic, parsley, and butter
Preserved California grown geese from Sebastopol
Vela dry Monterey Jack cheese from Sonoma
Fresh caramelized figs
Walnuts, almonds, and mountain pears from the San Francisco Farmers' Market

The menu is worth printing in its entirety because it contains several of the defining characteristics of the style. Here, English has supplanted French as the language that is used. Here, as the wine business had succeeded in doing, the "large" California has been replaced the "small" one of the "creek," the "bay," and the "farmer's market." And here also is the famous specificity of cooking techniques and ingredients and their provenance that may have started out as a call to quality but would soon lead to three lines on a menu being required to describe a salad and endless tableside recitations by waiters in oxford shirts. These recitations became such a national ritual that soon they were being parodied by late-night comics ("First we catch the lobster, then we tear off its claws, then we gouge out its eyes, then we immerse it in boiling water," one such waiter tells an increasingly horrified couple). And yet the comics' words, transmitted in the flickering light of television screens into millions of homes, made it clear that what was being parodied was not the style of a single restaurant with a honeysuckle hedge and a monkey puzzle tree fronting Shattuck Avenue in Berkeley, California, but something much larger, an entire aesthetic, a "gastronomic aesthetic" to reprise Olney's term. It is because a new aesthetic is the hardest thing to achieve in the restaurant business—the reason, after all, why restaurant trends come in waves—that there is still something vaguely unresolved about whether credit for creating it should go to Waters or to Tower.

⊢⊣

"AND THE DISH RAN AWAY WITH THE SPOON"

To ask that question of restaurant people in San Francisco and Berkeley is to enter into a hermetic world in which positions were taken long ago. As if signaling the dimension that opinions on the subject have taken on, they are invariably offered off the record. "Alice guards the myth very carefully," one restaurateur will say. "Jeremiah is envious of her success," says another. The San Francisco Chronicle came down noncommittally when it described the situation at the restaurant that led to Tower leaving as one "where a number of egos were tangled." After he left, a minor feud did develop between them, one that was mainly stoked by Tower. Waters seemed prepared to acknowledge his influence; for example, telling Newsweek in 1982 that "he taught me that you can really spoil food for people if you seem apologetic, that you have to appear confident even if you don't feel it." He perhaps felt that not enough people understood his influence on the restaurant. By 1984, the year he opened his own highly praised and successful San Francisco restaurant Stars, he was dismissing some of the culinary principles that he himself had helped forge as "very Berkeley."

Tower himself is not very Berkeley. His ideal of service is the one performed at Harry's Bar in Venice. His favorite if-ever-I-could-have-eaten-at restaurant is the legendary Alexandre Dumaine's Hôtel de la Côte-d'Or in Saulieu. His formative culinary experience was eating a *truite au bleu* with mousseline sauce in 1969 at Stonehenge Inn, the restaurant that Albert Stockli opened in Connecticut after he left RA. (Baum left in 1970 as RA began a long slide toward mediocrity that has since been reversed, making it once again a power in the American restaurant world.)

When I met Tower at Stars one evening, he seemed to embody that urbanity. He wore a well-cut gray-flannel suit over an ecru silk T-shirt and leaned sportingly against the polished brass rail that ran the length of the bar as he looked out at a crowded dining room. He had recently sold Stars—name, concept, and location—to an Asian developer and any feuds that may have occurred in the past seemed ancient history. (Though after he evinced interest in what Waters had said about him and I, perhaps indiscreetly, quoted her as saying, "The quality went up one hundred per cent with Jeremiah's arrival," he did seem pleased.)

After offering me what turned out to be the first of many glasses of champagne, he appeared quite happy to share with me his memories of the early days of Chez Panisse. My notes are an almost continuous quotation: "When we ran out of food, which happened a lot, we'd raid the walk-in and call it 'Walk-in Cuisine' . . . We'd run over to the Co-op for chickpea flour, which is disgusting, to make panisses which, just to complicate things, are not only a Pagnol character but also those little chickpea crêpes they serve in Nice . . . I'd get home maybe at one in the morning and at six I'd be at some meat jobber in Oakland explaining what an *onglet* was." It was all very vivid. And yet, as I wrote down what he said, I realized that despite his best efforts (and Waters's, too, and all the hours in the periodical section of the San Francisco Public Library), I was failing to connect with Chez Panisse. I wasn't actually seeing the place as any more than a series of direct quotations. It wasn't a real place to me, not the way, for example, the kitchen of Le Pavillon was. As the night wore on and the champagne took its course and the restaurant slowly emptied, leaving us sitting under the large Mistinguett posters with the busboys cleaning up around us, I finally admitted this to Tower. He smiled, perhaps acknowledging that both he and Waters had too much at stake to fully communicate what they knew. Then he reached over the bar, took what remained of the champagne, and, after splitting it between our two glasses, he sized me up as if deciding whether he really should be this helpful to me. "You should talk to Willy Bishop," he finally said.

"Who's he?" I asked.

"He worked with me in the kitchen for the first few years."

I quickly wrote down his name and waited for Tower to reach for an address book to give me his phone number. But the name was all he gave. "How can I contact him?" I asked. Tower knocked back his glass and signaled to the hostess who was waiting to close up that we were about to leave. "I'll put the word out," he said, and with that we stumbled out into the foggy night.

Contacting Willy Bishop by "putting out the word" suggested he was an individual who wasn't fully settled. It was an accurate impression. A few days later, when I called Tower, word of his whereabouts had not yet come back to him. Neither was he in the San Francisco, Berkeley, or Oakland telephone directories. In the spirit of the times, I was starting to refer to him, in my mind, as "Deep Palate" and had conjured up an idea of his being an unreconstructed product of the sixties—a man still living underground. A few days later, during a second call to Tower, he suggested that I use as a trail one of

Bishop's nighttime paths and call Jeannette Etheredge, the owner of Tosca, the old bar on Columbus Avenue in North Beach. I called her. "I haven't seen him for a while," she said, speaking loudly over the barroom noise. "I think he's working at Whole Foods in Berkeley and living with people from Chez Panisse."

The Whole Foods Grocery Store on Telegraph Avenue and Ashby is "deep Berkeley." As with the Co-op that preceded it (the place where the Chez Panisse crew would run for exotic ingredients like chickpea flour for the panisses), it manages to combine the purchase of groceries with a certain amount of holistic idealism. There is a masseur on duty in a booth behind the cash registers should any shopper feel a spasm of stress while standing in line. Ask for tea here and the ponytailed clerk will not only stop what he is doing and lead you to the tea selection, but then further try and help by asking, "What kind of tea? Teas do things, you know." Ask the manager if Willy Bishop is an employee and, if he is, what is his department and schedule, and you will be dispassionately studied for any giveaway sign that you are attached to the judicial branch of the federal government.

Early one morning, I underwent that treatment. After a long, deliberative pause, I was directed to the meat counter. There I spotted a small, elfish man with a close-cropped gray beard, wearing a white work coat and a black watch cap, who was placing skinned chicken breasts in the display case. "Excuse me, I'm looking for Willy Bishop," I said.

"I am he," he said, smiling puckishly.

"Jeremiah Tower suggested I look you up and Jeannette Etheredge told me where to find you," I said after introducing myself.

"I must be important."

"You are to me."

When I told him what I wanted to speak to him about he said, "Meet me at four o'clock at Chez Panisse. Being there will bring back memories."

He showed up punctually at four o'clock at the upstairs bar. He wore a houndstooth cap and a faded black T-shirt with *The Godfather* logo barely visible on it under a worn red-plaid flannel shirt and carried a rolled-up umbrella. "Should we get a table?" I asked, sensing that the proximity of the small tables at the bar would hamper his reminiscences.

"I'll just take one if I want," Willy said without self-aggrandizement but as someone who feels he's earned the right to sit quietly at a table that isn't being used. Before we could move, the host who'd been going over the evening's reservations came over to us. He was a man with close-cropped hair and wore expensive slacks and an acetate shirt buttoned somewhat fashionably all the way up to the top button. Willy introduced him as someone who had also worked at the restaurant in the early days. Then Willy mentioned that I was there precisely to find out about those days and almost immediately the man put his arm around Willy's shoulder. I felt it was done for my benefit, as a way of establishing the indulgent relationship he had with this colorful character—whatever he might proceed to say.

"Hey, can we get a table for a while?" Willy asked him.

The host made a face of regret. "They're setting things up," he said and quickly went off to get the herbal tea that Willy had requested.

"Things have changed," Willy said, and we remained sitting at one of the small tables by the bar.

After qualifying his remarks by saying, "I don't remember a lot of it, I was very high at the time," he proceeded, with a born storyteller's sense of pacing, to tell me much of what he remembered. Though he knew that it was Tower who had suggested I speak with him, I got no sense as he sipped at his tea that he was prepared to color his remarks for anyone's benefit. If indeed he was a refugee of sorts from the 1960s, he'd kept one of the era's most laudable aspects, which was a deeply held sense of personal integrity and an internalized code of ethics that he'd been able to maintain throughout the succeeding decades at no little cost.

With regard to how his own experience at the restaurant developed, he said, "I was the dishwasher. I never wanted all the responsibility. People would come in and try their hand at cooking and one night whoever was cooking was swamped and I helped them out and I became the chef's assistant." To set the scene, he said, "One girl worked with her tits hanging out. We kept a bottle of vodka in the fridge which we'd take shots of. Dealers would come into the kitchen and toss us an ounce of coke." To marshal this Dionysiac atmosphere, strong personalities were needed. Chez Panisse had them. "Nobody fucked with the French," was Willy's introduction to Tower. "It was Jeremiah's bravado, his posing, that made it possible. He's a Scorpio. Alice is a Taurus. She 'saw' it. One night we had a Moroccan dinner and we had braziers going on the ground and at the last minute Alice went running through the room spraying rose water in the air so the atmosphere would be just right."

For a moment, this image stayed with me. It captured a certain innocence that was sometimes hard to perceive behind the restaurant's famous name. I looked at Willy as he spoke and it suddenly struck me as meaningful that I had contacted him through Tosca, because I'd recently come across a reference to the bar in *Last House*, the posthumously published book of recollections by M. F. K. Fisher. In 1943, she'd written, "Then she drank, after one or two brandies at La Tosca, an Americano, a sage biting mild drink. She looked down the bar at all the thirsty people. There were two soldiers getting ready either to beat up two dainty civilians next to them or go to sleep. . . . In the air over the sound of Nino Martini on the jukebox, she heard the foghorns blowing, and she thought of all the men wait-ing below-decks and of all the dog tags dangling on the warm-skimmed ribs."

This was only two years after Parrish's suicide and she was clearly still living the life of a "ghost." It was a sense that would never really leave her. Reading her, one comes to suspect that she strove to create a physical reality because she passed so lightly through life. If the place was real, then she must be too. Many of her books commu-nicate this, but perhaps none more completely than *Map of Another Town* (1964), the book she wrote on Aix-en-Provence. "I feel some-what like a cobweb there," she wrote in the characteristic timbre of her writing. "I do not bother anyone. I do not even wisp myself across a face, or catch in the hair of a passerby, because I have been there be-fore, and will be again on my own map." This is a form of existential travel writing. Its goal is not to know all the interesting facts about a town but to create a reality out of the flotsam and damage of one's own life.

Though Fisher lived for many years in Glen Ellen in Sonoma County north of San Francisco (and died there in 1992), her somewhat reserved nature kept her from participating too fully in the food movement she'd played such an important role in creating. She was slightly too edgy to blindly join in the countercultural enthusiasms of the Berkeley food world (when *she* went to the Vieux Port she wore long white gloves) while her sense of verbal punctilio made her recoil at the rhetorical excesses that often accompanied the enjoyment of food. "Very nice people have told me," she wrote in the *New York Re-view of Books* in 1979, "that some things they have read of mine, in books or magazines, have made them drool. I know they mean to compliment me. They are saying that my use of words makes them oversalivate, like hapless dogs waiting for a bell to say 'Meat!' to them."

But much greater than the differences she might have had

with the young cooks of Berkeley was the shared emotional require-
ment to create one's own reality, to will a place into existence. Thus,
for Fisher, in trying to re-create Aix, it was less important to be at the
local museum taking notes than every evening on the same café terrace, with the same Campari and soda before her, looking down the
double row of plane trees of the Cours Mirabeau. Similarly, for Alice
Waters, if her restaurant was to be the kind of restaurant she'd
dreamed of, it was imperative, if the occasion demanded it, to run
through the dining room spraying rose water in the air in the moments before the customers arrived.

Willy was still talking. "We were manic," he said fondly. "Alice would be over with Ron Fuji, who owned the produce store on
Shattuck, carrying on in her tiny little voice about the tiny little vegetables she wanted just like they had in France, because none of the
purveyors understood her vision. Jeremiah would come back from
Chinatown with a six-foot-long conger eel for the bouillabaisse." It
was the first time I'd sensed the actual solidarity that must have existed between the restaurant's principals for it not to have collapsed,
like so many similarly idealistic restaurants of the time did, into a
crossfire of recriminations, a heavy-handed use of sprouts, and an in-
ability to get an order to a table.

"What we pulled off unknowingly," Willy said, smiling
vaguely in my direction, for the tea had grown cold and he seemed to
be swimming in the years. "Once it was set, once it was Chez Panisse,
it was easy."

The moment of transformation, the institutionalization of
the name, might be said to have occurred with Caroline Bates's
Gourmet review of October 1975. The review was so good it would
have transformed any restaurant. The irony was that the staff and
friends of the restaurant took it to be the beginning of the end. Chez
Panisse would no longer be the intimate, undiscovered, restaurant
they had known. Darrell Corti, the food and wine merchant from

Sacramento and the restaurant's institutional memory, sent the Mafia's black funeral wreath. Willy Bishop, to the accompaniment of the phone's suddenly ringing off the hook because of Bates's review, suggested that they "Do what she liked three times. These turkeys will come in with the review in their hands." Far from the Vieux Port now, Chez Panisse had reached the inescapable stage of restaurant success in this country: how to deal with crowds.

WOOD-FIRED

Young restaurant PR director: *"I kind of like the lull between seatings."*
Joe Baum: *"NEVER like the lull."*

—Joe Baum in conversation.

PIZZA LOGIC

In *Fin-de-Siècle Vienna*, the historian Carl E. Schorske argues that the reason Vienna at the turn of the nineteenth century was such a culturally influential city was precisely because it wasn't Paris, London, or Berlin, but rather "the little world in which the big one held its tryouts." Cooking French food in Berkeley was not akin to cooking French food in New York which—like singing an aria in Milan or dribbling a soccer ball in Rio de Janeiro—was an activity on which half the city felt entitled to hold an opinion. In Berkeley, there was an atmosphere where one could experiment and make mistakes, and where an educated and indulgent clientele understood that the cooks were working their way toward a style.

Once that style was formulated, however, there was a conjuncture of the idea that young Americans were reinventing French food (for that is how it was often described), the unexpected discovery that anything of culinary interest could come out of California, the rise in quality of California wines, and the increased power of the gastronomic press that made for an amalgam that was not only highly promotable but also highly promoted.

The new aesthetic was communicated cleverly through events. The first and most influential was the annual Four Seasons California Vintners Barrel Tasting dinner, which was organized by wine dealer Gerald Asher together with old RA hands Tom Margittai and Paul Kovi, who had purchased the restaurant in 1973. Though the event began in 1976, and thus predates the recognition of the culinary developments that were coming out of California, precisely because it was held at the Four Seasons, truly an epochal American restaurant, one perhaps reads more into it than one should.

Were the laconically named dishes that Chef Seppi Renggli turned out—oyster cassoulet, essence of duck in crust, sautéed Wellfleet scallops, for example—the ultimate detoxification of the American culinary vocabulary of all French pretension? Was there a symbolic dimension to the fact that Alexis Lichine, who once upon a time would have dismissed California wine as "a bottle business" (as opposed to the more profitable "case business"), was now one of the guests holding forth on the wonders of a particular Californian varietal? In this same vein, was it the ultimate proof of the promotability of California wine and food that spotted in the crowd, sitting together at table nine, sipping at their flight of Diamond Creek Cabernet Sauvignon while nibbling on Sonoma goat cheese were the two demigods of promotion, Sam Aaron and Joe Baum?

The template of promotability thus set, other events quickly followed. A 1978 event held at Tavern on the Green to which Alice Waters brought her little rocket lettuces with their roots still in soil and her chef, Jean-Pierre Moullé, carried in the Dal Porto Ranch lamb over his shoulder is, in the chronology of the movement, generally acknowledged to be the moment when New York got to see what the new Californian food was all about. A 1980 event held in Newport, Rhode Island, where Jeremiah Tower cooked an entire meal, including dessert, in little black pans on a grill for over one hundred syndicated food writers, is the way that knowledge of the style was disseminated throughout the country. While a 1983 dinner held at the Stanford Court Hotel in San Francisco in honor of James Beard's eightieth birthday brought together many of the principals of what had by now become a movement.

In addition to Waters and Tower, here was Larry Forgione of the River Café in Brooklyn serving terrine of three American fish with their respective caviars. Here was Jonathan Waxman of Michael's in Santa Monica preparing red pepper pasta with grilled scallops. Paul Prudhomme of K-Paul's Louisiana Kitchen in New Orleans set up out on the fire escape so that the searing of all the blackened catfish for the banquet wouldn't set off every fire alarm in the hotel. Mark Miller of the Fourth Street Bar and Grill in Berkeley prepared marinated grilled quail with poblano chile, cilantro, and lime sauce. And Bradley Ogden and Jimmy Schmidt, respectively of American Café in Kansas City and, Beard's old favorite, the London Chop House in Detroit, joined forces for the main course of roasted rack of lamb stuffed with Missouri greens and hazelnuts, gratin of wild root vegetables, fiddlehead ferns, and cattail sprouts. While such meals certainly proved that the principles of specificity that had evolved out of California could be applied to other regions, there was also something self-fulfilling about the very success of the events at which those meals were served. In other words, the more customers that were converted to the style, the more the style was going to have to adapt to feed them. The chef who cooked one of the two dishes served at the party that followed the Beard dinner was the one who realized it first and most successfully. He served Spago pizza and his name was Wolfgang Puck.

A more unlikely chef to be the transforming force could not

be imagined. Though Austrian, Puck was steeped in the French tradition. He'd worked at L'Oustau de Baumanière in Provence, where Roger Fessaguet of La Caravelle had worked. He'd also worked at the Hôtel de Paris in Monte Carlo, from where Marius Isnard, the original chef of the French Pavillion in Flushing, had come. He'd been night chef at Maxim's on the Rue Royale, the very epicenter of *le standing*. When Puck took on the job of chef at La Tour in Indianapolis, he was so unprepared for his new country that he thought the city might be similar to Monte Carlo, since both had grand prix car races.

Situations like that were not rare in the culinary world to which Puck belonged. One went where one was paid. When Puck arrived in the United States in 1973, he was one of many chefs in that tradition. Georges Perrier, an *ancien* of Baumanière, too, and also of La Pyramide, where he'd risen to *saucier*, had worked at La Panetière in Philadelphia for three years before opening his own Le Bec-Fin in 1970. Another alumnus of La Pyramide, Jean Banchet, had worked at the Playboy Club in Chicago before he, too, opened his own restaurant, Le Français, in Wheeling, Illinois. These were the hired guns of the culinary world; men who could perform such feats of culinary virtuosity as sending out one hundred hot soufflés—simultaneously. It was another member of this fraternity, Pierre Orsi, today of Lyons, but then the chef of a sister restaurant of La Tour, The 95th, on the ninety-fifth floor of the John Hancock Center in Chicago, who got Puck his green card. As soon as he got it, he headed for Los Angeles.

The city Puck arrived in in 1975 was just beginning the transformation by which it would eventually supplant Berkeley and San Francisco as the place where the most interesting culinary developments were going on. Within a few years, the age of Perino's, Romanoff's, La Rue, and Chasen's would have given way to the one of Michael's, Trumps, L'Orangerie, and La Toque. Even so, what gave Puck the confidence to stay in Los Angeles and try his luck was not the endlessly repeated bromides about how the California cuisine that had come out of Chez Panisse was being taken even further in the city. It was the career of one particular man, a man who had come out of the same tradition as Puck, Jean Bertranou.

Bertranou, who, tragically, would die in 1980 at the age of fifty of a brain tumor, was chef and owner of L'Ermitage, a place that looked like a little French country house located on La Cienega Boulevard. It was the very focal point of culinary LA, the place where Paul Bocuse cooked special dinners when he came to town. While the success L'Ermitage enjoyed gave Puck confidence that the city could appreciate the culinary level at which he'd been trained to perform, it was Bertranou's personality that captivated him most. Bertranou, originally from a hamlet near Pau in the Béarn region of southwest France, was alive to the ironies of working in his adopted country. He'd worked for mobsters at the Sands in Las Vegas. He'd taken that old standby, veal chops Orloff, possibly as far as it could be taken by preparing it on La Cienega Boulevard, a street that had working oil wells. He bred ducks with Michael McCarty of Michael's in a farm in the high desert, where the silence was occasionally interrupted by the explosion of an illegal methamphetamine lab. This was no chef complaining that it wasn't France and that the products weren't any good and that he couldn't wait to save enough money to get back to France. This was a chef who was very much here and thriving in the strange situations that working in the American market could produce.

Ma Maison, the restaurant where Puck soon became night chef and co-owner, was also capable of this combination. Located in a freestanding house on Melrose Avenue, Ma Maison and its very fame depended on the combinations it managed to produce. Its unlisted phone number was known by all of Hollywood. The Rolls-Royces were parked by the garbage containers in front of the restaurant. While the other co-owner, Patrick Terrail, was a member of the family that owned La Tour d'Argent in Paris (he'd begun his American career by being a plate-checker at the Four Seasons), the floor at Ma

Maison was famously Astroturf, and worn Astroturf at that. It was here that Puck found a home. He turned vegetables, wrapped oysters in lettuce leaves, and added to the general off-kilter air that reigned in the restaurant by serving *canard en deux services* to such good customers as Robert Rauschenberg and Irving Azoff, the manager of the rock group the Eagles. (Thus establishing, surely, the only known link between the hyperclassic way of serving duck breast and leg over two courses and the Eagles' hit "Desperado.")

His wife and business partner, Barbara Lazaroff, met him at this time. He was living, she likes to recall, in a room with sheets over the windows and an *Emmanuelle* poster on the wall. This was the flip side of being a hired gun. You cranked out the exquisitely crafted nouvelle cuisine dishes, then returned to your darkened room. It was also at this same time that the strangest transformation took place in Puck. It was something that wasn't supposed to happen to hired guns, something that had previously happened to Jean Bertranou and which had drawn Puck to him as a friend: Puck was influenced by his environment. The chef who'd worked at Baumanière and the Hôtel de Paris, the chef who had been so uninterested in his environment that he had thought Monte Carlo and Indianapolis might be similar, was influenced by California.

At first, it was in the expected way, by getting caught up in the promotional vortex that surrounded California food and wine. A 1981 event for a California winery (held at Windows on the World the same week as the Four Seasons' Barrel Tasting to take advantage of the heightened coverage) shows Puck working within the parameters of the California style. The wines that were being promoted were Jordan Vineyards' '79 Chardonnay and '77 Cabernet. The menu that Puck had devised included caviar from Columbia River sturgeon, pigeon from Carpenter Ranch in Santa Barbara, and Sonoma goat cheese from Laura Chenel. But giving the provenance of ingredients was being influenced by California only in the most superficial way. California was working on Puck on a different level. He was starting to think of food in a pre-professional way. The food he wanted to cook in the future would provide fewer opportunities to display technical mastery but instead be characterized by simplicity and, yes, even for this most classically trained chef, an emotional dimension.

Cooks will often display some of their emotions on a menu. The very term *après* is an homage to people who've influenced them or to legendary cooks. Puck was French enough to do this. His insistence that there always be a marjolaine on the dessert cart at Ma Maison can be interpreted as a tribute to Fernand Point and, by extension, an allusion to the great French provincial restaurants that were the ideal of Ma Maison (but which the Astroturf floor at times failed to convey). Similarly, today on the Spago menu, there is a whole section devoted to "Wolfgang's Childhood Favorites," which includes such evocative dishes as giant farmer's cheese ravioli with hazelnut brown butter and spicy beef goulash with sautéed spaetzle, parsley, and marjoram. Where one sees best the emotional importance he attaches to food is in his cookbooks when he talks about the bouillon with bone marrow, the mashed potatoes of his childhood, and most of all the bread. His books are filled with anecdotes about the making and baking of this most basic and spiritual of foodstuffs: the neighbor who made huge rye loaves, the way his mother would sprinkle water on slightly stale bread before placing it in the oven for a few minutes. Clearly Puck was a professional chef capable of undergoing what might be called the "M. F .K. Fisher at Mazatlán Airport" effect, when food went from something with an "outer" value to something with an "inner" one.

He had reached this stage by the time he started looking around for a location for his own restaurant. At first, he was going to open it with Patrick Terrail, but after a disagreement he decided to go it alone. He found the space perched above Sunset Boulevard in the restaurant that had been Kavkaz. (The one Caroline Bates had admired for the "smoggy charm" of its view.) In his privately printed memoirs, the restaurant's owner, Yervand Markarian, gives an account of a life lived in the Armenian Diaspora. "As a family man, I owned and managed restaurants in China, Brazil and California—all of them Russian/Armenian and all of them called Kavkaz," he writes on page two. Toward the end of the thin volume, as he prepares to sell, he describes what his Los Angeles restaurant had given him and his family. "We had a nice home in Glendale," he writes with a touching simplicity, "a first class/popular restaurant and could for the first time in our lives feel that we were settled and 'belonged.'" Amid all the lamb specialties of the restaurant, its strolling violinists, and the Cossack dances that would occasionally break out, Markarian had been able to define himself to his new country. In 1982, when it was Puck's turn to do the same, he chose not to be one more practitioner of the already dying fashion of nouvelle cuisine but to define himself by serving food that had an emotional meaning for him—by making pizza.

The story one hears most often about Puck's interest in opening a restaurant that served pizza is that when he was an apprentice at Baumanière, he and his fellow cooks would eat on their days off at a pizza joint in town called Chez Gus. The story then proceeds to touch on how Puck was influenced by the pizza oven that Alice Waters had installed in the upstairs café at Chez Panisse in 1980. (She, in turn, had been influenced by the oven at Tomasso's in North Beach, which even as gas pizza ovens became the norm had continued the tradition of pizzerias from North Beach to New Haven to use woodburning ovens.) In 1982, Puck had the same German bricklayer that had built the Chez Panisse brick oven build an oven for him. (The man is still remembered for drinking cases of beer up on the scaffold and disposing of the empties by including them in among the bricks.)

The story is cute. It has a nice continuity and is undoubtedly true. But chefs that are making *canard en deux services* one year are not tossing pizza dough the next on such simple grounds. True, making pizza the dish the restaurant would be known for joins a true professional chef's delight in simplicity with a nothing-left-to-prove level of confidence. But something else is going on with the opening of Spago. By the time it happened, Puck, with the broad frame of reference that his culinary background gave him, had spotted some of the ironies that had always existed at the heart of the California style.

The most obvious irony was that many of its practitioners felt that there was something original about putting American place-names to a culinary use. Nothing, in fact, could have been older. As Evan Jones's monumental *American Food* makes clear, the use of regional place-names in dishes such as New England baked bean soup goes back to Colonial days and thus is older than the Republic itself. Even if one takes the practice of using place-names simply for their promotional value, it dates at least as far back as the nineteenth century, when Maine oysters, Maryland terrapin soup, and canvasback duck from the Chesapeake marshes were important component parts of what Lucius Beebe called "5th Avenue cuisine circa 1895."

A second irony is that the Chez Panisse style was often referred to as "cuisine bourgeoise." Similar to such terms as "cuisine de bonne femme" and "cuisine du terroir," "cuisine bourgeoise" is one of those culinary styles whose name resounds deeply within the canons of French gastronomy but whose precise definition is often difficult to pin down.

The late André Guillot, whose restaurant outside Paris, l'Auberge du Vieux-Marly, is remembered as the apogee of the bourgeois style, dated the inception of the culinary principles he practiced to the eighteenth century and in particular a book entitled *La Cuisinière bourgeoise*. Published without an author's name in 1793, its goal was to describe modified versions of the dishes previously enjoyed by the aristocracy for the cooks of the new élite, the bourgeois. Closer to our own time, the Culinary Institute of America's *The New Professional Chef* describes the style simply as "the cooking of hearth and home." While the eighteenth century serves to give historical context and the twentieth to give a latter-day adaptation, it is the nineteenth century—what historian Eric Hobsbawn has called "the bourgeois century"—to which we must turn in hope of understanding the style.

The nineteenth-century bourgeois was nothing if not riddled with anxieties. There was a provincial anxiety. In French literature, its defining moment may be the opening scene of Flaubert's *The Sentimental Education*, in which young Frédéric Moreau is leaving Paris by boat and, as the quays fall away, realizes the dread with which he's facing the coming two months he's to spend in the country. There was a social anxiety—Proust's Baron Charlus incessantly referring to the habits of the bourgeois, to the extreme discomfort of the very bourgeois narrator, would have to define this. The bourgeois even managed to have a culinary anxiety. Obsessed with status, and thus inordinately conscious that he had servants to perform housekeeping duties, the true bourgeois would not even go into the kitchen. Indeed, the distance from the kitchen to the dining room was an index of the size of one's house (another one was the number of staircases it contained) and consequently of one's position on the constantly monitored scale between haute and petite bourgeoisie. (By way of bourgeois fantasy, the kitchen and dining room at the Rothschilds' estate at Ferrières were linked by an underground train.)

In the final analysis, cuisine bourgeoise is perhaps the only culinary style that might be best defined by a moral sense, one that all bourgeois shared, that of thriftiness. It is best represented by cheap cuts of meat that require long cooking times. In contrast, grilling, the cooking method that came to define the California style was fast and required expensive cuts of meat. *Boeuf à la mode* (Proust) is cuisine bourgeoise. Grilled Niman-Schell Ranch beef tenderloin (Chez Panisse) is not. Lamb neck you put into a *navarin*, lamb loin you grill. Thus, the California style wasn't only not cuisine bourgeoise; it was its very antithesis. (It is only fair to note that it was journalists and not Waters who made the cuisine bourgeoise claims. She even tried to counter it, allowing to *Newsweek* in 1982 that "stews and this restaurant have never really mixed.")

Caroline Bates touched on a third irony in her original review of Chez Panisse. To her surprise, the dishes that she enjoyed so much were not cooked by "someone who had followed the traditional route of the *chef apprenti*, progressing from pot scrubber to *saucier* in some respectable restaurant in France." As one consequence of this, sauces had never figured prominently at the restaurant. The irony, for a restaurant so committed to capturing the essence of French cooking, is that sauces are French cooking's highest achievement. *Poivrade*, *grand veneur*, *chasseur*, *bordelaise*, *Nantua* . . . sauces define all the subtlety and balance that are its glory. Great sauces demand great skill and a commitment of time. A great *saucier* will choose his bones carefully: never use pork or salmon bones for a stock because their taste is "fat." He will brown the bones in great roasting pans until they are the perfect color. He will degrease with infinite care. He will compose his mirepoix seeking ultimate balance, not too many carrots or onions because they will sweeten the stock, not too much celery because of its pronounced flavor, this all the way down to the ingredients of the bouquet garni, where neither thyme nor bay leaves should dominate. A great *saucier* criticizing an apprentice's sauce will not start by criticizing the sauce but by criticizing the stock with which the sauce was made. If your menu is changing daily, as it was at Chez Panisse, you might not necessarily want to invest the time a great sauce requires if you can use it for only one meal. If you were in college and not, like a *saucier*'s apprentice, forced to stay in the kitchen to skim the stocks in the afternoons, you may not even want to try.

But Puck had been a *saucier*'s apprentice. He did have the hard-earned touch. Sauces were precisely the culinary tradition he came from (best illustrated by the traditional chef's knotted white

napkin he wears around his neck in his early pictures). He had to decide consciously not to make them the focal point of his restaurant.
While Spago did make veal stock and the menu had a red wine sauce
and a port wine sauce among others, Puck made every effort to promote the restaurant as one in which traditional sauces were not the
selling point. "Everywhere there is beurre blanc with fish," he is
quoted by Bates as saying in the original Spago review. One interpretation of this is simply that he wanted to position the restaurant outside the nouvelle cuisine style; but another reason, a deeper one, has
roots that are as personal as they are professional.

I had been trying to meet Wolfgang Puck for several weeks to
interview him for an article I was writing. Hours before each scheduled meeting, I invariably received a phone call from his office can-
celing the meeting because he "had to fly to Las Vegas" or "was fogged
in in San Jose." One rainy day, I simply went over to Spago Beverly
Hills after the lunch service and asked to see him, and before I knew
it, he'd materialized, apologized for all the confusion, and showed me
to a quiet table by the courtyard so that we could finally talk. The rain
dropped through the branches of the olive tree at the courtyard's center and Puck asked a waiter to bring me a cappuccino. I could see he
was tired. He was clearly putting the best possible face on having to
do yet another interview and I sensed he might actually get up and
leave if I were to mention the words "smoked salmon pizza." To
change the dynamic, I mentioned that in addition to freelancing for
magazines, I was working on a book on the history of the American
restaurant business. The moment I did, Puck asked me a question.

"Who was Louis Diat?" he asked as if it were something that
had been on his mind for a while.

I told him what I knew. That he'd been chef at the Carlton
House and Ritz Hotels in New York since 1910 and had been famous
for his vichyssoise and had retired some time in the 1950s. I added a

fact that I'd recently read, that his nephew had been chef *saucier* at the French Pavilion in Flushing and later, as a member of the French Resistance, had died at Belsen. Also, that his brother Lucien had been chef at the Plaza-Athénée in Paris, where a young Jacques Pépin had worked under him. He nodded with interest and then we started the interview proper, but I had the sense that the world of Diat hung over the entire conversation. It was as if I'd said, "Diat was a man trapped by a time and by a dish." It was a position that was not uncommon for chefs with Puck's background and one that he had made great efforts to break out of.

I mention all this as a preamble to calling Puck ambitious. As someone who grew up without much money, he had every justification for wanting to be financially rewarded for his enterprise. Unapologetically so. "I am very happy with what is happening to chefs," he told the *Los Angeles Times* in 1978. "I am very happy that chefs can drive Rolls-Royces." He is the only chef of the California movement who could actually say this. Unlike the rest of them, he had not come to cooking after his education but at the price of his education. He went to great effort not to spend his life behind a stove because spending his life behind a stove was a very real possibility. He didn't want to be trapped in a job, or by a dish, or to be given a gold watch by any hotel company. He wanted to reposition the entire profession of chef. To be able to do that, he needed not one but many restaurants. If he were going to be a star chef, appear monthly on *Good Morning America*, have to fly to Las Vegas, be fogged in in San Jose, he needed a culinary system that didn't require the technical ability that he himself had.

The California style handed it to him and this was its greatest irony: for all the creeks, hills, arroyos, ranches, farms, coasts, bays—the small world that its vocabulary invoked—it was actually tailor-made for the American mass market. If you grilled a lot, kept the sauces simple (didn't have to find a skilled *saucier* every time you opened a restaurant), and promoted pizza (a dish whose production, once the recipe is set, doesn't actually require the possession of a palate), you were making the many restaurants that you envisioned operating much easier to staff. You had taken sound culinary principles and adapted them into a system that, with the right financing, could be endlessly reproduced.

My last cooking was in a restaurant that ruthlessly exploited the essential simplicity of the system Puck had devised. Its catch-all style was "Mediterranean." We could serve six hundred people in one service. Two phrases I heard at that restaurant will always stay with me. The first was said by a line cook working the rotisserie, who one night, as the orders for ducks kept coming, finally called out to the chef, "I'm going to keep cutting ducks until you tell me to stop." When you have no idea of where the food is going, you've lost control of volume.

The restaurant's chef and owner said the second phrase to me when I interviewed for the job. "Maybe you're the sort of guy who keeps demi-glace in his freezer," he said, leaning back in the chair in his office, "but we're not." The intimation was that demi-glace, the constantly reduced and skimmed essence of veal stock that gives backbone to many traditional sauces, was somehow old hat. Instead, he kept a stock kettle going at all times into which all kitchen scraps were tossed. He claimed that this was the way it was done in the farmhouses and quayside cafés of the Mediterranean. Since no one ever bothered to skim it, its surface did indeed have a detritus-filled frothy cap similar to the one that tends to form around the hulls of boats moored in ports such as Tunis and Genoa—but that was its only Mediterranean aspect. In reality, he didn't want sauces because veal bones and veal feet for a veal stock had to be bought and weren't simply by-products of the kitchen and because he didn't want to pay a member of his staff to make something when that person's time could be put to much more profitable use, generating income on the line.

His favorite sauce was *romesco*, the Catalan red pepper and almond sauce that is often served with grilled fish. He always found something to serve it with. Anyone, no matter his or her skill level, could be given the measurement of the ingredients and instructed to place them all in an industrial-sized blender. Not only did ten minutes' work provide sauce for an entire service; if he was talking to journalists, which he often did, *romesco* gave him the opportunity to drop the name of Elizabeth David.

To hear him justify his "grill and garnish" operation with the name of Elizabeth David made me want to literally shake him. It was Elizabeth David without heart. Puck without skill. I grew so depressed I became careless. Well into our five hundredth cover one night, I laid a damp (thawed, of course) rabbit loin into a pan of hot oil. Instead of doing it correctly, laying it from front to back so that any oil that splashed out would go away from me, I laid it quickly from the back of the pan toward me. A jet of oil shot out of the pan and up my forearm. One of the young line cooks (who thought they were learning cooking there) took my place. I numbed the pain with a spray from the first aid kit and caught a cab to the hospital. Sitting in a bucket seat in the emergency room waiting for my name to be called, I looked down at my blistered and swollen forearm. Then I looked at the worn houndstooth cook's pants I wore and at the grimy combat boots into which they were tucked. For some reason, this combination, together with the shock of the burn and the suspended nature of time spent in an emergency room, made me see clearly that I wasn't going back. Not to that restaurant or any other. I wasn't only burned, I was burned out. I'd always wanted to write. It was time to start.

The system that Puck devised worked perfectly for him. One year after opening Spago, he opened Chinois on Main, a restaurant that superimposed a Chinese influence over the preexisting and perfected Spago formula. Today, he operates many restaurants, including several Spagos and Wolfgang Puck Cafés that offer an entry-level version of his style. In recollections of the opening night at Spago, one already hears the tone of something inevitable having begun. Mark Peel, today the co-owner with his wife, Nancy Silverton, of Campanile in Los Angeles, but then part of the tiny opening-night crew, perhaps captures it best. "It was Nancy on pastry, Wolf on grill, Ed was working pizza, I was working pasta, and Kazuto was on pantry," he says, describing kitchen stations in the rapid-fire speech pattern that is the lingua franca of busy restaurant people. "We kept the menus open on the counter so that we could remember what the ingredients were and whatever presentations we came up with that night were the Spago presentations for years afterwards. We were so busy that we'd go through a cord of wood a week. That's four feet high, four feet wide, and eight feet long. A tractor-trailer would come down from Northern California every three months and they had to time their arrival for four in the morning so they could negotiate the hairpin turn off Sunset and they'd unload it in the parking lot."

The café at Chez Panisse also went through a cord of wood a week. And yet there is a world of difference between its being unloaded off Shattuck Avenue in Berkeley and its being unloaded off Sunset Boulevard in Los Angeles. In Berkeley, the restaurant was a short distance from the Co-op; in Los Angeles, it was a short distance from the Chateau Marmont (where John Belushi overdosed and died). In Berkeley, it was a further development toward a culinary aesthetic, in Los Angeles, that aesthetic had made contact with the full power of the American market. The wood-fired age had arrived.

"CHE TI DICE LA PATRIA?"

In 1982, when Isidoro Gonzalez saw Julia Child waiting in the line that forms outside La Super-Rica Taqueria in Santa Barbara, he wasn't sure what to think. He knew she was a great woman and that she was a wintertime resident of the coastal California town and that she'd taught Americans all about French food. But why was Julia Child, her husband, Paul, and two other friends here among the day laborers and students who start to arrive almost as soon as the restaurant opens at eleven every morning?

The answer is that they wanted precisely what everyone else who goes to La Super-Rica wants: the *chorizo* that's charred on the grill, the *tacos al carbón*, the tortillas that a woman working beside the grillman presses to order, the *gorditas* that are roasted quickly over an open flame, the cool *horchata* drink that blends rice water and cinnamon, and the freshly cut *pico de gallo* with onions, cilantro, and tomato that is placed in an earthenware bowl at the end of the counter where the other homemade garnishes are kept. When the line had snaked along and it was their turn to order, Julia Child stooped her tall shoulders, leaned in toward the window, and, in the endearingly high-pitched voice in which many Americans had first heard the words *"Bon appétit!,"* she asked for *"un poco de todo."* A little of everything.

The country had changed since 1961, when Child's *Mastering the Art of French Cooking* had been published. Child and her co-authors had intended the book to break the stranglehold "easy" French cookbooks held on the market. The success with which this was achieved caused it to become the new culinary style manual for the housewives who counted among their many tribulations entertaining their husbands' boss. With the disappearance of such constricted social roles— and the America that required the corresponding manuals—a deeper facet of the book becomes clear. With typical Childian subtlety, this is not spelled out but implied. In the recipe for *petis pois frais à la française*, Child writes, "This dish is considered the glory of pea cookery; it should really be served as a separate course and eaten with a spoon." Now serving a single course of peas with a spoon to the boss and his wife was not going to grease the wheels of any husband's career. But the book had never been intended to do that. What made *Mastering the Art of French Cooking* a groundbreaking book was not so much that it was an authentic French cookbook as much as that it was an authentic cookbook that happened to be French. It was an understanding of food that allowed its author to go into raptures over a butter-infused serving of fresh peas with pearl onions and just-cooked Boston lettuce quarters. But also to wait her turn in line at La Super-Rica Taqueria with the town's gardeners in their jeans and baseball caps and order her tacos and take her tray and eat them on the canvas-roofed patio bordering the dirt parking lot in the back.

What makes La Super-Rica "worth the detour" (exit highway 101 at Milpas and go north about a mile) is that it is an ethnic restaurant that sells authentic ethnic food. Paradoxically, the two have not always gone together. This was not done out of some wish to sell counterfeit goods but because the underlying goals of an ethnic restaurant—to employ as many members of one's family as possible and from time to time send money back home—were never conducive to experimentation. Whatever formulation of a national cuisine had proven itself to be successful to an earlier generation of immigrants was the one that more recent arrivals were most likely to repeat.

A whole new take was required to reposition ethnic food outside the immigrant experience. This, tellingly, was not achieved in restaurants but through cookbooks. The amount of ground that had to be regained was often reflected in the stridency of their tone. "To me the word 'curry' is as degrading to India's great cuisine as the term 'chop suey' was to China's," Madhur Jaffrey wrote in her 1972 book, *An Invitation to Indian Cooking*. "But just as Americans have learned, in the last few years, to distinguish between the different styles of Chinese cooking and between the different dishes, I fervently hope that they will soon do the same with Indian food instead of lumping it all under the dubious catchall title of 'curry.' 'Curry' is just a vague, inaccurate word which the world has picked up from the British, who, in turn, got it mistakenly from us. It seems to mean different things to different people. Sometimes it is used synonymously with all Indian food. In America it can mean either Indian food or curry powder. To add to this confusion, Indians writing or speaking in English use the word themselves to distinguish dishes with a sauce, i.e., stewlike dishes. Of course when Indians speak in their own languages, they never use the word at all, instead identifying each dish by its own name."

Jaffrey's book was one of a veritable minimovement of ethnic cookbooks published in the early and mid-1970s that strove to take ethnic cooking out of the realm of the cliché. George Lang's *The Cuisine of Hungary* presented Hungarian food without the Gypsy violinists. Claudia Roden's *A Book of Middle Eastern Food* and Paula Wolfert's *Couscous and Other Good Food from Morocco* took Middle Eastern and North African food beyond the realm of belly dancing. Cecilia Sun Yun Chiang's *The Mandarin Way* introduced her readers to "northern style" Chinese food without reverting to any of the dragon lady nonsense in which so many other Chinese cookbooks came packaged. A particularly telling name in the acknowledgments of Diana Kennedy's seminal *The Cuisines of Mexico* is that of Elizabeth David, "who was, unwittingly my inspiration, for when I first went to Mexico I read and cooked from her books avidly." That one could extract principles from *A Book of Mediterranean Food* that could be applied to the food of Mexico makes clear that even though all these books championed an indigenous authenticity, they held certain underlying principles in common. Despite the paprikas, the ghee, the epazote, the bisteeya, the tamarind paste, and the fried jao-tze that separated them, they shared a unifying aesthetic, one that might indeed be called Davidian, of unmannered sophistication and rusticity.

If rusticity was the direction food was to take, then it could easily be thought that Italian food would have had a head start. Certainly, if the opposite of rusticity was taken to be French haute cuisine. The tenets of haute cuisine of limpidity, distillation, and smoothness stand in direct opposition of those of Italian *cucina*. Where the Italians might grill a whole fish over dry vine shoots, the French must pass a fish mousse twice through a *tamis*. Where the French must chop their parsley to its finest consistency, the Italians might add their herbs whole or cut fairly large. *Ébarber*—to strip mussels of the black lip that surrounds them; *émonder*—to seed tomatoes; *tailler*—to shape vegetables: in haute cuisine, you always must be doing something to the product. The problem for Italians was precisely that their best food stood in direct contrast to the aesthetic of refinement that was the ideal throughout the 1940s, 1950s, and 1960s.

The cookbooks of the time are dispassionate evidence. In

sickly green Ektachrome shots, one gets to study pictures of what looks like the staggeringly long buffet table of some bad hotel on the Lido. The trussed pheasants lie on soggy deep-fried croutons, there are mayonnaise constructions and decorative cornichons fanned out *en éventail*, and langoustes *en bellevue* that just barely manage to stay upright. Perhaps saddest of all are the chicken breasts *en chaud-froid* in which the béchamel has been so loaded with gelatin that it has set before it has even had time to coat the meat. The chefs are obviously straining. Straining with effort, straining most clearly to be French.

The shadow of France would prove very difficult to escape. Even such passionate interpretations of Italian food as Angelo Pellegrini's *The Unprejudiced Palate* (1948) seek to define *cucina* in terms of cuisine. "It is idle to insist that the mature cuisine of one country is better than the equally mature cuisine of another. French cookery is generally preferred to all others for no better reason, I think, than that, as in all things where coteries and cults seem to be the fashion, the French have seized and never relinquished the initiative. Some prefer the Italian because its pretensions are modest and worth achieving, while its happy blending of the leguminous and the farinaceous, the emphasis on green vegetables, and the sparing use of meats make it eminently satisfying as a steady diet."

This may well be true, but the "happy blending of the leguminous and the farinaceous" was not going to get anyone thinking, "This, I have to eat." It wasn't until 1973 and the publication of Marcella Hazan's *Classic Italian Cookery* that a book appeared on the American market that put Italian food in terms that were neither dietary (like Pellegrini), touristy (like *Italian Bouquet* of 1958), or sentimental (*Mama Leone's Italian Cooking*). Hazan came out of the same revisionist mold as many other cookbook writers of the 1970s. Like Jaffrey and Kennedy, she had been giving cooking lessons in her New York apartment for several years before the publication of her book, and the book fully captures the authoritative tone that made her classes so popular. It opens with a veritable broadside across the bows of every red-leather-boothed "Italian" restaurant in America. "The first useful thing to know about Italian cooking is that, as such, it actually doesn't exist. 'Italian cooking' is an expression of convenience rarely used by Italians." After describing the regional differences that exist in Italy and describing the many small courses that go into an Italian meal, she too turns to the shadow of France, but it is not to define herself or her book by it but rather to finally dismiss the comparison. "The best cooking in Italy is not, as in France, to be found in restaurants, but in the home. One of the reasons that Italian restaurants here are generally so poor is that they do not have Italian home cooking with which to compete. The finest restaurants in Italy are not those glittering establishments known to every traveler, but the very small, family-run *trattorie* of ten or twelve tables that offer home cooking only slightly revised by commercial adaptations. Here the menus are unnecessary, sometimes non-existent, and almost always illegible. Patrons know exactly what they want, and in ordering a meal they are evoking patterns established countless times at home."

The publication of Giuliano Bugialli's *The Fine Art of Italian Cooking* in 1977 developed Hazan's thesis by going into fascinating detail on the ambiguous meanings of the word *povera*. "In Tuscany," he wrote, "the word 'povera' meaning 'poor' is sometimes used, in a form of reverse snobbism, to mean 'genuine' or 'good' when referring to food. The implication is that nothing sophisticated or unnatural is used." There are many examples in the book, but one in particular is notable for the way the use of a single ingredient can throw a switch in an entire understanding of a country's food. The dish was *risotto ai fagioli con l'occhio*, risotto with black-eyed peas. Black-eyed peas! Here was an ingredient that Americans not only knew but also could place within a known culinary style. In fact, with a growing realization of where this was headed, one could even start pairing off ingredients.

Cannellini beans were black-eyed peas, broccoli rabe was mustard greens, pancetta was salt pork, polenta was grits: no wonder Italians loved their *cucina povera* so much, it was their version of soul food!

Thus, increasingly liberated from stereotypes, Italian food began its transformation. Its lack of pretensions contrasted favorably with the caricature of French food that had developed over the years. It was healthy and cheaper, and its image dovetailed nicely with the Tuscanification of the general aesthetic. Today, Italian restaurants bob up and down the avenues like moored fishing boats. We can all discuss which one offers the best version of *polpettone di vitello* (previously known as meatballs), and principles of Italian *cucina* have so deeply penetrated the American palate that in most urban centers, a waiter bringing a plate of olive oil for dipping to a table is not even considered a foreign custom anymore. Where the popularization of Italian food became most evident to me was not in a restaurant at all but in a place where much of the produce that they require is grown: Salinas, California.

Salinas is "the town that iceberg lettuce built." In season, the refrigerated warehouses are lit up all night and the great chambers where the air is extracted from the packed boxes are constantly pushing out loaded pallets to be lifted into waiting eighteen-wheelers for trips to all points of the United States. In 1988, Lucio Gomiero first came to investigate the possibility of his farming in the area. He found the richness of the soil and the banks of fog that in the evenings came down over the shoulders of the Santa Lucia Range that separate the Salinas Valley from the Pacific reminiscent of his native Veneto. It was, he decided, the perfect place in which to grow Italian vegetables, and most specifically radicchio.

On the afternoon that I drove around Lucio's fields with him in his all-terrain Mercedes truck, he showed me huge tracts of *cavolo nero*, the Tuscan cabbage used in the bread soup known as ribollita;

and whole beds of *cime di rape*, the turnip tops that cooked together with *orecchiette* pasta and seasoned with a paste of anchovies and browned garlic is a traditional dish of Puglia, the heel of Italy. He showed me when he called "an experiment" (to explain why he still wasn't growing it in huge quantities) of *puntarelle*, wild chicory spears that look like asparagus tips growing out of thicket of dandelion greens. Then, driving closer to the Gabilan Range that marks the eastern border of the Salinas Valley, we came into the broad fields of radicchio.

One side of the muddy path the round, tight *chioggia* heads that are used in salads were grown; on the other side, the long thick-ribbed *treviso* variety that is used for grilling. "We're working on *castelfranco*," Lucio said, referring to the pale, freckled variety which, like Belgian endive, has to be "forced" in darkness and which, like *treviso*, is named after a town in the Veneto. "There's more *treviso* in this field," he said looking out over its expanse, "than the entire town of Treviso could produce."

Later that night, lying in bed at the local Comfort Inn, listening to the loaded rigs rev their engines as they entered the freeway, I found myself thinking about what Lucio had said. There was more radicchio in one American field than in the entire Italian town the vegetable was named after. I realized to what an extent American volume could transform anything it touched and it clearly had had that effect on Italian food. But to reach this point of success, it first had to escape from under the shadow of France. While authors such as Hazan and Bugialli could lead the way with their books, for it to be understood by a larger group, it had to be put into practice. Paradoxically, it had to be done where the shadow of France had been most dominant, in a restaurant. Balzac himself in the *Comédie Humaine* could not have better plotted that the restaurant where this would happen would have no homey Tuscan touches at all; its design, in fact, was based on the *singerie* at Versailles, where the King of France kept his pet monkeys. It wasn't located in any stronghold of Italo-American food, San Francisco's North Beach, South Philly, Boston's North End, or New York's Little Italy, but on the Upper East Side of Manhattan. It didn't even have an Italian name. It was called Le Cirque and its owner was Sirio Maccioni. Because he was an Italian and the food he served was predominantly French, it brings into focus the long-simmering tension between French and Italian food. Because it was one of the most exclusive restaurants in the country, it is the perfect prism through which to look at the ever-shifting notions of American class. What might be called *le standing*, phase two.

THE MAN FROM MONTECATINI

Sirio Maccioni slipped in behind the range. He watched a young cook—who suddenly appeared to be extremely nervous—cut into a rack of lamb. When the cook had finished plating the lamb, Maccioni, thinking he couldn't be seen from the dining room, picked up the last bone that had been left on the cutting board and happily chewed off the meat. He wore a beautiful, elegant blue suit, a blue shirt of a shade that a playboy rather than a banker might wear, and a blue tie with large polka dots, a cheerful motif he favors and which, it being Le Cirque, recalls the baggy overalls worn by circus clowns. Finished with his middle-of-the-service snack, he wiped his fingers on the towel hanging from the cook's apron string and headed back out to the dining room. It was a real restaurant person's gesture: to be the owner of a restaurant and not wish to break the rhythm that a line cook develops in the course of a service by asking them to make something special. To be Sirio Maccioni and to take the small leftover bone of a rack of lamb before it is grabbed by a passing waiter or a dishwasher come for dirty pots.

The scene was the new Le Cirque 2000, located in the gilded rooms of the Villard Mansion in New York. McKim, Mead and White, the preeminent architectural firm of Edith Wharton's New York, built the mansion in 1882 for Henry Villard, a railway and publishing tycoon. Due to business reversals, Mr. Villard was not able to indulge for too long in his particular whim of residing in a replica of Rome's Palazzo de la Cancelleria, located on Madison Avenue and Fiftieth Street. Since he sold it, tenants and owners have included Ambassador Whitelaw Reid, Random House, the Chancery of the Roman Catholic Archdiocese, hotelier Harry Helmsley (who attached it to a hotel), and the Sultan of Brunei. If all this amounts to a microcosm of the tectonic shifts that have affected New York society and provides a link between *The Age of Innocence* and our own coarser age, it is appropriate that Sirio Maccioni in his cheerful polka-dot ties should be the ringmaster at its center.

If ever there was a right restaurant for this location it is Le Cirque, a restaurant whose own pedigree came straight out of the Colony Restaurant. The Colony, in its post-Prohibition incarnation, became popular the day after Mrs. Vanderbilt chose to eat there. Similarly, the tables under the famous blue-and-white-striped awning became the red-hot center of café society the day after the Duke of Windsor said to owner Gene Cavallero, "We'll dine here, Gene, the bar has such a gay atmosphere."

For all the fine restaurant lineage Maccioni could invoke, there is something genuinely unaffected about him. Put simply: he is not a snob. He may be unable to resist purring "Ah, the untouchables" in the direction of a table with a particularly high glamour quotient, but he has little patience for people with airs. In tours of the dining room, he is more likely to have a kind word for the woman who has checked her coat rather than for the one who insists on blocking a path between the tables with her draped chinchilla. To acknowledge the young man looking awkward in a tie and to ignore—this master of the retinal dismissal—the one whose exaggerated gestures are simply meant to display the working buttonholes on the sleeves of his custom-made suit.

In conversation, similarly, he makes every effort to counter the impression of snobbery. "What is a maître d'," he likes to say, "but a pretentious waiter." Or "These cooking schools today, they are so luxurious I want to go there on vacation." One writes them down the first time that one hears them but not the second. One subject on which Maccioni's conversation truly engages is on the subject of Italian food. "I was importing radicchio in 1974," he'll say with some passion. Or "I always put good Tuscan olive oil on the tables for people who knew. I made some mistakes. People would say, 'Sirio, it can't be any good, it doesn't have a label.'" Or "So much Italian food today, it is cooking without a past!" He is heated, he is ruffled, it is almost as if one has brought up something personal. And in many ways, one has.

The matrix of Maccioni's character was laid in the watering holes of café society in Europe in the 1950s. In conversation, there is often a streak of place-names where he has worked (which are delivered in that rapid-fire stream of consciousness that is Sirio-speak, which one knows better than to slow down for clarification). These invariably include the Dolder Grand Hotel, Zurich, the Palace in St. Moritz, the Plaza-Athénée in Paris, and, always, the Grand Hotel and La Pace in his native Montecatini Terme, where in 1948, as a young teenager, he began his dining room apprenticeship.

What this background trained him in was not only the techniques of Russian service—*présenter, découper, recomposer*; or present, carve, recompose—but also, just as important, the tastes of café society. What the clientele he was trained to serve liked was subdued lighting, banquettes, paillards for lunch, soufflés for dessert, and, above all, to be recognized when they walked in. This was not hard. It was a small world. "The people you saw in Montecatini in spring," he says, "you saw in St. Moritz in winter."

He was providing these services at La Forêt at the Hotel Pierre in 1973—the Colony, where he'd been maître d'hôtel having closed—when he was contacted by real estate developer William Zeckendorff, who wanted to open a restaurant at the Mayfair-Regent on Park Avenue and Sixty-fifth Street. Together with Colony chef Jean Vergnes as partner, they opened the new restaurant on March 20, 1974. The opening-night menu included *bar rayé poché beurre blanc*, *entrecôte au poivre vert*, and *soufflé au gingembre*. A whole world is implied in that menu: the people one saw in Montecatini in spring and St. Moritz in winter may have enjoyed their maître d's being Italian, but they wanted their menus to be French.

Maccioni would never claim that the popularization of Italian food that has taken place in this country since the 1970s should be traced to him. That is a subject that, in New York alone, would have to include many different facets of Italian food. To name only a few, the restaurants of Mulberry Street would represent the immigrant version, Romeo Salta's town house in the 1950s embodied the first wave of Italian sophistication, Tony May's San Domenico, on Central Park South, the second wave. Lidia Bastianich's Felidia, with its emphasis on the little-known cooking of Istria in the northern Adriatic, championed Italian regional cooking at its most diverse. But Le Cirque played an important role also. The early menus of Le Cirque include dishes such as *carpaccio toscane* and gnocchi and, as at the Colony, *bollito misto* was one of the weekly *plats du jour*. But no dish confronted the French supremacy that reigned in restaurants such as Le Cirque as much as pasta primavera. It may not have been the purest interpretation of *cucina* but it generated a huge amount of coverage, which in terms of a national cuisine trying to change its image was just as important.

The story of pasta primavera brings up the inevitable contrast between Maccioni and Soulé. They shared many characteristics: the merciless sizing-up, the essential shyness ("I'm reserved, even shy if you want," Sirio will allow), their tendency to revert to their native tongue in moments of anger, their fundamental lack of airs, and their total control of their dining rooms. Their greatest similarity may be philosophical; as Soulé did, Maccioni sees himself as the guardian of the most elegant tradition of dining. It is precisely this role that has led him to have, just as Soulé had, a conflicted relationship with the food that he himself likes to eat. Where Soulé would "whisper" about *plats bourgeois*, Sirio would put Tuscan olive oil only on the tables of people he thought would appreciate it.

The creation of pasta primavera—a dish that confidently announced itself as Italian—came out of one of the great professional differences between Sirio and Soulé. While Soulé was endlessly involved in strikes and walkouts by his staff and never allowed Pierre Franey into the dining room during a service, Sirio actually likes the company of cooks. Particularly when they get together outside the pressures and tensions of their restaurants and open up their wood-handled Opinel penknifes and slice the saucisson and splash out the red wine.

It was precisely under such conditions that a group of New York's most celebrated chefs would gather at the home of the painter Ed Giobbi in Katonah, outside New York City, in the early 1970s. On any given weekend, they could include Pierre Franey, Roger Fessaguet, Jacques Pépin, Jean Vergnes, even front-of-the-house people like Sirio and civilians such as Craig Claiborne and James Beard.

In addition to being a painter, Giobbi was also an accomplished cook—and cookbook author—whose food was the antithesis of the refined style in which his professional chef friends were trained. Giobbi canned his own tomatoes, grew his own vegetables, made his own wine, and, during summers on Cape Cod, canned his own tuna. It was a way of life that reminded many of the French chefs of the rustic backgrounds that they themselves came from. No less a Francophile than Claiborne would write, "Some of the most memorable meals of my life have been taken in Ed's kitchen." Beard, likewise, wrote that his lunch of homemade wine and bread and stuffed veal breast with Marsala and *verdura mista* was "one of the most enjoyable lunches I had in a long time, cooked as Ed believes food should be with a free hand, creatively using the freshest ingredients you can get."

At just such a gathering, Giobbi combined some fresh spring vegetables with pasta and Vergnes saw a dish that he might like to adapt for the restaurant. Back in the kitchens of Le Cirque, his first reaction was to make it more French. A little cream instead of olive oil, a little Gruyère instead of Parmesan, and, of course, a French name, *pasta aux primeurs*. At this, Maccioni stepped in. He lobbied for a return to Parmesan and he insisted on calling it "primavera." Calling it *aux primeurs* may have been more logical, a bow to the atmosphere of refinement that held sway at Le Cirque. To instead put it in Italian, to *insist* that it be in Italian, was an act of semantic self-assertion that to customers may have meant very little, but for a man who as a dining-room *piccolo* of sixteen had had *présenter, découper, recomposer* drummed into him, it meant the world.

Something else that meant the world to Sirio was maintaining the exclusivity that the restaurant tradition he practiced was founded on. However, he was not one to take it quite as seriously as Soulé, so his relationship with the general public was rather more flirtatious, presenting a meal at Le Cirque as a summit that they could actually aim for. It was an approach that perfectly complemented the style of restaurant coverage in New York throughout the 1970s and 1980s that revolved as much around power and glamour as it did around food. In the *New York Times*, the potential gastronome could keep up with reviews, trends, and techniques. *W*, a large-format, glossy sister of *Women's Wear Daily*, dealt with the glamour, specializing in lunch scenes and keeping its readers apprised on whether Jackie O had sat facing in or out at Mortimer's, who hit the social home run at La Grenouille, and who rode the banquette at La Caravelle.

The power school of restaurant coverage was the domain of *New York*. Under the editorship of Ed Kosner, who himself liked to lunch at the legendary Forty-sixth Street steakhouse Christ Cella, readers of the magazine got to see detailed seating plans of restaurants they might not be able to enter. The prototype of these articles, Lee Eisenberg's "America's Most Powerful Lunch," about the lunch scene at the Four Seasons that appeared in *Esquire* in 1979, put it succinctly: "Unless you're very persistent—or lucky—this is as close as you'll get." (Wouldn't you know it, Sam Aaron managed to get photographed for the article lunching with his friend Ab Simon, the all-powerful chairman of Seagram's fine wine division, Chateau and Estates.) In the same way, readers of *New York* got to read "Power House," which did its rendition of the grillroom's lunch scene. "The Power of '21' even included architectural floor plans of the restaurant. "High Noon at Le Cirque" covered a single lunch service and came with pictures of who was sitting with whom.

Sirio still laughs about that article. "From that day on I put anyone carrying a magazine facing the wall," he says, intimating that the pictures of his customers were taken secretly with a spy camera. In fact, Sirio had obligingly packed the house with his best customers and allowed the photographer, Harry Benson, who was known by many of the subjects, to stand on a chair in the middle of the dining room so that he could better capture the atmosphere. In other words, the photo shoot didn't happen surreptitiously; Sirio practically produced it. It might be considered his contribution to the long tradition of Cavallero, Soulé, and Beebe, which maintained that the best way to get people in was to plant in their minds the idea that they might not be able to. His way of toying with the alternating currents of access and restriction that would always make the atmosphere at Le Cirque feel charged.

"Walked over there and we got the worst seats," Andy Warhol wrote in his diaries about a visit to Le Cirque in 1981 to watch Ronald and Nancy Reagan eat. "We couldn't see anything, so Franco took the best seats and he started describing to us every little thing the presidential party was doing. All of the tables had reporters having dinner to cover the president, the whole place was foreigners. Bob and I were the only Americans. Then we were leaving and I didn't want to go by the president's table because it was too groupie-ish—everybody else was stopping by the table—so we went the other way, but they called us over, Jerry Zipkin was yelling and I met Mrs. Reagan and she said, 'Oh, you're so good to my kids.'"

This is a nice example of the sort of scene, always one social somersault away from a three-ring riot, that Sirio has managed to orchestrate sometimes twice a day for over twenty-five years. He is our own age's practitioner of the oracular, "This way, please." With greater frequency, there may be a lieutenant or one of his three sons at the door to do the actual greeting, but it is his image that is positioned between one standing nervously at the door and sitting happily at a table. When he himself leads the customer to a table, the journey across the dining room becomes a form of inverted perp walk that demonstrates fame rather than infamy; demonstrates above all that one is known. Because being known at Le Cirque has taken on dimensions that do not too fully correspond to logic—and led to the suspicion that not being known is grounds for receiving an inferior level of service—the restaurant has proven to be an irresistible target for restaurant critics, whose very authority increasingly has come to depend on their anonymity.

It wasn't always so. Rereading Craig Claiborne's original review of the Four Seasons one is struck by a phrase he used in describing a particular dish. "Typical in the cold selection," he wrote, "is an 'herbed lobster parfait.' If memory serves, this contains large chunks of lobster enrobed in a devastatingly rich blend of whipped cream and hollandaise sauce." What resounds in one's inner ear today is not the dish but the phrase "If memory serves." We are so accustomed to the tone of reviews being one of absolute certainty that we are struck by this note of uncertainty. Did he not take the note? Did his mind wander as the dish was presented? Had the wine kicked in? Had he simply forgotten? Was he human? The forthrightness of the expression and the fact that he would admit rather than fake his recollection of the dish is indicative not only of Claiborne's stylistic self-assurance but also of the unconflicted ethics of restaurant reviewing in 1959.

As reviewing increasingly came to be done by ex–food consultants and sometime feature writers (who might need the people they reviewed today for a quote tomorrow), the greater became the need for them to demonstrate their independence to the reader. The wigs, the hats, the sunglasses, that they wore and soon became the stuff of urban legend made a point that was as symbolic as it was practical. They not only didn't go when they were called. They also weren't recognized when they went.

Mimi Sheraton, who reviewed restaurants at the *New York Times* from 1976 to 1983, practiced this refusal of access at its most ascetic degree. The fact that she'd worked for Joe Baum as a food consultant for the Four Seasons did not prevent her from describing a club sandwich eaten at his Windows on the World in 1976 as "acceptable, perhaps, if sent up by room service in an out-of-the-way hotel." Inversely, the fact that she was the scold of New York restaurateurs did not prevent her from leaping to their defense. In 1979, when the *New Yorker* printed a story in which a certain "Otto" claimed that

Lutèce used frozen fish, she sicced herself on the case. André Soltner himself was prepared to simply show his fresh fish receipts to anyone who cared to see them, but Sheraton wasn't content to leave it there. Together with a *Times* stringer and the paper's wine reporter, Frank Prial, they had soon tracked "Otto" down at the small Pennsylvania restaurant that he ran. For his troubles, the man found himself the subject of a Sheraton review. "The truly awful first course was composed of slices of briny, pale-yellow artichoke bottoms of the type usually canned, topped by large chewy gray snails that tasted dank and musty." The overall impression: "It's not that he isn't an honest man serving honest food. It's just that his dishes are badly conceived. He doesn't have a palate." Anyone else with unsupported allegations?

Sheraton was that marvelous combination of the right reviewer at the right time. The single page devoted to "food fashions family furnishings" on which Claiborne's reviews had appeared had by then become a whole newspaper section. The talk of fiddlehead ferns and sauce pointillism was verging on the hysterical. The "As close as you'll get" school of restaurant coverage had become a city's obsession. At the center of the storm was Sheraton, the most important critic in the country, who managed to observe it all with the cocked eyebrow of one of Brooklyn's own. She didn't care whether it was high noon at Le Cirque or not. Her reader was on the 5:45 out of Grand Central—and the Friday 5:45, at that. With typical dryness, she described the atmosphere of Le Cirque as "a game of performers versus spectators, pure and simple, though apparently worth playing for those who enjoy watching the famous and the fashionable." Yes, there was a scene, one that she was not necessarily beyond but outside. It was her way of communicating New Yorker to New Yorker with her reader. A restaurant critic's way of saying, "I'm working here!"

As much as she kept New York restaurateurs on their toes during her reign, it was a pair of articles on dining in France that perhaps encapsulates her approach best. Appearing in June 1979, they described in detail her findings on a five-week eating tour of France. The first paragraph of the first article set the tone. Her advice was to "take boxes full of cash (credit cards are rarely accepted at top restaurants) and realize that while it can still buy some of the world's best food, it can also buy a higher percentage of disappointing meals than ever before."

She went on to delineate exactly why. Except for a few high moments such as at Lameloise in Burgundy, her opinion was low. She trashed the bread (often where a Sheraton review starts), the level of service, the "inexcusable background music," and, most pointedly, the very movement through which haute cuisine sought to reinvent itself, nouvelle cuisine. "Most deplorable of all, perhaps, is the epidemic of the nouvelle cuisine—the 'new cooking' devised by Bocuse, Troisgros, Guérard and company. At its best it is refreshingly light, natural and delicate, but it all too often becomes a substitute for real skill."

This was read not only on the 5:45 out of Grand Central but in France. In fact, it caused such a furor that she was invited to appear on French television along with Bocuse and several other personalities from the food world. The TV executives who dreamed it up may have planned on its being one of those calm, deliberative sessions of which the French are inordinately fond. But with Bocuse and Sheraton at the same table, this was hardly likely to be the case. Bocuse was furious that his movement had been attacked, by, of all things, an American. As for Sheraton, well, where she came from, even if you were wearing a wig and a veil to hide your face, you just didn't back down.

The scene is perhaps best captured by *People*, who thought enough of the confrontation to cover it ("Who's Killing the Great Chefs of France? Mimi Sheraton Proves They Can Dish It Out But Can't

Take It"). "Before taping began, Bocuse had puffed up his cheeks and waddled around in an ungallant impersonation of the critic," *People* reported. Afterward he'd lunged unsuccessfully for the wig and the veil. "I expected him to do something like that," she said later. "Only I thought he'd do it on TV. I'm sorry I didn't hit him in the face."

This is surely the restaurateur-critic relationship at its most aggressive. But there is something symbolic in the gesture of a chef as well known as Bocuse grabbing for Sheraton's symbols of anonymity. It's the aggression of a confused man, as if the American critical enterprise has interjected a hybrid of criticism with which he is unfamiliar. Here was an anonymous critic, but one who was sitting across a table from him. The *Guide Michelin* critic was anonymous also, but one didn't get to puff up one's cheeks and waddle after them. Inversely, the guide that set itself up as the alternative to the *Guide Michelin*, the *Guide Gault-Millau*, was named for two journalists whose faces were known to most chefs in France and were not given to dining anonymously.

In fact, it was quite the opposite—they announced their arrival. On August 10, 1984, Christian Millau came to a long lunch at Restaurant Guy Savoy, then on the Rue Duret in Paris, where I was working. We knew what he would be eating in advance. I still have the menu written down and it still represents, for me, the simultaneous rendition of subtlety, rusticity, and sophistication that is French cooking at its best.

Amuse Bouche: *Écrevisses en gelée de lapin au Sauternes.*
[*Dom Perignon*]

Huîtres en Nage glacée
Étuvée de St. Pierre à l'huile d'olive
Charlotte d'Homard
Rouget Poêlé à l'estragon
[*Chevalier-Montrachet '78. Leflaive*]

Ragoût de Champignons Sauvages
[*Haut-Brion '53. Magnum*]

Salmis de Pigeon
[*Haut-Brion '61*]

Fromage
[*Latour '53*]

Glace Vanille, Coulis d'Abricots
Tartelette de framboises

For all I know—minion that I was—this wasn't a meal intended to be criticized but a celebration of someone's birthday. (The two '53s might be indicative of that.) For all I know, Millau kept it on the up-and-up and paid for the meal. What I do know is that as soon as the last hot course left the kitchen, Savoy beamed like a gymnast who has stuck a landing, a chef under no doubt that this great meal would go into the tally of his yearly toques by which the guide rated restaurants. This was the situation that American critics had to resist constantly. It wasn't access. It was access with magnums of Haut-Brion. Access at its most venal.

Since the possible corrupting influence of access was a constant presence in readers' minds, it perhaps was only a question of time before a system was developed that made corruption a logistical impossibility. The *Zagat Survey* provided that system. Begun in 1979 by Tim and Nina Zagat as a restaurant-rating newsletter for friends, the guide's incorruptibility was based on having frequent diners fill out questionnaires and mail them back to the *Zagat* offices for tabulation. The sheer number of respondents—by the time *New York* did an article on "The Food Spooks" in 1985, they numbered fifteen hundred—provided the statistical accuracy.

But the methodology had a flaw, one that the ratings of Le Cirque might well illustrate. The questionnaire that was sent out urged respondents to rate the restaurants at which they ate by food, decor, service, cleanliness, and cost and to add under comments any "pithy quotable reactions" that they might have. The guide rated the quality of the food cooked in Le Cirque's kitchen—under the successive command of Alain Sailhac, Daniel Boulud, Sylvain Portay, and Sottha Khunn—consistently high. But the atmosphere in the dining room was somewhat harder to pin down. For several years running, this "yearly" guide included in its description of the restaurant the phrase "the place to go if you want to go where it all is." This phrase wasn't exactly pithy, in fact, its sheer repetition intimated that as democratic as the *Zagat* system was, and as fair as the tabulated results could be trusted to be, "pithy quotable reactions" were not easy to come by. To really nail a scene, one needed an old-fashioned undemocratic reviewer, one with an inimitable voice and a full arsenal of rhetorical devices, one like Gael Greene or Ruth Reichl.

Describing Le Cirque as "a soup kitchen for the anguished orphans of the late Colony" has a voice. It also has attitude. The phrase is smart enough, the choice of words charged enough, the attitude confrontational enough, and the social dimension evident enough for the knowledgeable review reader to immediately recognize this as Greene (writing on Le Cirque in 1977). What it isn't is informative enough, and that, too, is Greene. For her, the considered opinion was always expendable before the nicely turned phrase. In 1965, writing in the "New York" section of the Sunday *Herald Tribune*, she described Soulé in action thus: "He carries his five-feet-five inches as if they were ten, withers offenders wordlessly with owl-eyed disdain from behind round tortoise-shell-rimmed glasses, and moves with the speed and purpose, although with not quite the style, of Jean-Paul Belmondo." With similar gusto, there were few occasions on which she could resist indulging in a Beebe-like taste for alliteration (for her, "money" didn't go with "Mornay" but "flageolets" did go with "flagellation").

On the plus side of the ledger, she fairly eviscerated the entire context in which restaurant articles were written. No longer were they acts of collusion with grateful restaurateurs but statements of solidarity with snubbed patrons. In this new adversarial relationship, the legions of fans who read her in *New York* could root for her as she showed them "The Menu Rap and How to Beat It," "How Not to Be Humiliated in Snob Restaurants," or "How to Melt the Glacial Sommelier." With its felicitous phrasing and headlong pacing, there was a seamless quality to the Greene review at its best that would have been very difficult to top. Ruth Reichl would not try to. As modern as her references were, her style actually reverted to an earlier time. Like Claiborne's "if memory serves," she let the reader see the seams. She wasn't a disembodied opinion. She was always someone who had to write a review.

Though Reichl was a native New Yorker (the mandatory RA connection was that as a child her parents would take her to see, but not eat at, the wonders of Forum of the Twelve Caesars and La Fonda del Sol), her style was formed away from the city. After studying sociology at the University of Michigan in the late sixties, she began a westward drift that eventually led her to work at the Swallow, a collective restaurant at the Berkeley Art Museum. With time, she would begin reviewing for *San Francisco* magazine and following that for *New West* and *California* magazine (in which she memorably captured the atmosphere of early Spago as feeling "like Paris in the twenties, a floating crap game, and your eighth birthday all rolled into one"). Her tenure at the *Los Angeles Times* ended in 1993 when she was tapped to replace Bryan Miller as the restaurant critic of the *New York Times*. She returned to New York fully formed. Her California years had marked her. Just as Sheraton's combative style might be said to be reflective of her Brooklyn roots and Greene's style revealed the national interest in sophistication of the Kennedy years, it was Reichl's Berkeley years that would most strongly mark her style.

There are several aspects in which this is so. Two of them touch on the subject of access. The first is that a Berkeley background demanded a certain level of transparency, whether in politics or restaurant reviewing. If access existed, it had to be admitted. And Reichl did. "I look at my friend, Alice Waters, who owns the now famous Chez Panisse, and see the dilemma of success," she wrote in a 1983 article entitled "Homesick at the Nouvelle Restaurant." "Alice's restaurant has grown so famous [that] others are trying to copy the formula, and the recipes they follow are all wrong. For Chez Panisse has not been successful because it is serving the world's finest food. It has been successful because it is serving what people most want and need: love, attention—and good food."

This not only stresses an emotional understanding of the dining experience (another Berkeley trait that would mark Reichl's style) but also is an instance of a restaurant reviewer unapologetically welcoming the insight that access allows. Not because there might be some Haut-Brion in it for her, but because it contributes to the reviewer's most important duty by adding to the reader's understanding.

The second aspect of being a reviewer who "comes" from Berkeley is that one constantly finds oneself either trying to get into or eating at restaurants where one really feels one doesn't belong. For Reichl, this situation often became the dramatic hook for the entire piece. As with any good drama, it required dialogue. A 1981 review in New West of the Los Angeles landmark Chasen's is a good example. After watching the antics of a succession of "playboys, producers, preachers and politicians" she poses the key question to the waiter. "'Does this happen all the time?' . . . 'Not really,' he replied, listing the many dignitaries and political types who had dined that night. 'I guess you get all kinds,' I answered, 'from royalty to riffraff.' He put his arm around my shoulder and said reassuringly, 'I wouldn't call you riffraff, sweetheart.'"

This is a nice twist on the access question. Refusing it or accepting it doesn't come up. You don't have to pretend to be no one— you *are* no one. It is also a persona for a critic to have developed that is literally bursting with comedic possibility. It wasn't until she trained her sights on Le Cirque in 1993 as the *Times's* new reviewer that it was used to its full potential.

Reichl's first review appeared on September 3, 1993, and she put her dialogue technique to good use by opening with the dismissive replies she received at certain unnamed restaurants. "'Lunch for two?' There is a vague snicker. 'Not a chance. We're booked for weeks . . .'" (The snub as a review's lead—that got the reader's attention.) By October 8, she was proving her culinary bona fides by taking on La Grenouille. (Again she opened with dialogue: "'What's the difference between restaurants here and in Los Angeles?' is a question I am often asked by people who know I have spent the last twenty years thinking about California food.

"'La Grenouille' is my answer.")

By October 29, less than two full months after her first review, she was standing nervously at the front door of Le Cirque. Like so many before her, it was by this restaurant that she would define herself to her readers. The review was divided in two parts. In the first part, she described the treatment she received before anyone realized who she was. The crucial line of dialogue here being delivered by a waiter: "'I need that wine list,' he says, peremptorily holding out his hand." The second part described the treatment she received once she was recognized for who she was. Only Sirio could deliver the perfect opening line here and he certainly came through. "'The King of Spain is waiting in the bar,'" he said, spotting her in the crowd at the door, "'but your table is ready.'" It was a line that, in essence, she'd been preparing her entire career to hear.

The King of Spain is constantly being dragged into reviews of Le Cirque. Bryan Miller painted the scene by opening his 1992 review with: "Truffle sandwiches and Tiffany trinkets, King Juan Carlos and crème brûlée." The *Zagat Survey* commented on "the political seating" one could experience at Le Cirque, explaining that "when the better table goes to Nancy R or Juan Carlos you can't get too offended." The reason the King of Spain is mentioned so often is because he is a customer of the restaurant and a friend of Sirio's. It is a relationship about which he is not reticent. The King of Spain this, the King of Spain that, it is almost a conversational tick for him.

The thing about Sirio mentioning the King of Spain is that it is not name-dropping. Niarchos handing out hundred-dollar bills to anyone in a dinner jacket one night does that. As does Frank Sinatra sitting in a corner eating his well done *milanese*. Nixon getting a standing ovation in the dining room. Stories that involve Henry Kissinger, Mick Jagger, Andy Warhol, Barbara Walters, *bref*, Sirio has name-dropping covered. No, when Sirio mentions the King of Spain, he is giving a glimpse deep into his own personality. It is Proustian, an invocation not of wealth or power but "Society." It is not name-dropping at all but a natural reflex for someone with his background. There was absolutely nothing that the people one saw in Montecatini in spring and St. Moritz in winter admired more than a king who would eat at a restaurant. It harks back to the future Edward VII's carriage speeding off what was the Avenue d'Antin—today the Avenue Franklin D. Roosevelt—and swinging around the huge lilac grove that hid the private entrance of Le Petit Moulin Rouge, where Escoffier worked. It is, after all these years, *le standing*.

On September 14, 1998, Sirio was at it again. The scene was the Villard Mansion's Belleville brownstone courtyard. The occasion, the party for Le Cirque's twenty-fifth anniversary. Mayor Giuliani's announcement that it was officially "Sirio Maccioni Day" went off without a hitch. But that was the last thing that did. When it was Sirio's turn to talk, he was so overcome with the emotion of being surrounded by his many friends and loyal customers that he was unable to follow the notes he'd prepared on the back of an envelope. Not being able to follow his notes is a bad thing to happen to Sirio. Suddenly ad-libbing, he found himself touching on subjects as diverse as his barber back in Montecatini and the regrets sent by the King of Spain. It was his entourage that brought him back to the point. Yes, there was indeed an announcement to be made (one that with Sirio speaking on a stage under a huge video screen showing the fake lake of the Bellagio resort in Las Vegas came as a surprise to few): Le Cirque was opening a branch in Las Vegas. With that, he introduced the chairman of Mirage Resorts and the mastermind behind the Bellagio, Steve Wynn.

Straight off the bat, Wynn struck one as a man unfamiliar with the sensation of having a microphone ripped from his hand. But this is exactly what happened during his speech when a playful Bill Cosby grabbed it (in a gesture that suggested he had seen enough footage of the man-made re-creation of a Northern Italian lake that separates the Bellagio from Las Vegas Boulevard) and fairly shouted "Let's eat!" Steve Wynn understood. Cutting his remarks short, he signed off by inviting all present to a free stay at Caesars Palace, one of the casinos in Las Vegas that Mirage Resorts doesn't own. With that insider joke, he stepped off the stage, flashing a pearly smile.

Everybody was smiling. Sirio's three sons, tight around Papa. The members of the staff doling out the prosciutto and melon. The circus juggler who greeted the limousines on Madison Avenue. The young cook with a whisk in each hand whipping the zabaglione in copper bowls. The hundreds of friends who'd turned out for the party. Only Sirio seemed, for a split second, daunted by precisely what had just been announced. Le Cirque was opening a branch in La Vegas. Say that slowly. The untouchables were going to meet Siegfried and Roy. The restaurant that required a jacket and tie was going to the city where long pants were considered going formal. The tradition of the French court was going to meet the tradition of the food court. Bridging historical eras by serving pheasant à la Souvarov to people going on to Studio 54 would seem like a positive cakewalk compared to this. But there was no point thinking about it. Still in the friendly confines of the Villard Mansion's Belleville brownstone courtyard, he launched himself into the crowd while an accordionist took his place on stage, cocked his hip in the best *bal musette* style, and launched into "La Vie en Rose" as if there were no tomorrow.

But there was. A month later, in the Bellagio's Monet Ballroom—down the carpeted corridor from the Bellagio's wedding chapel—when Sirio came to meet the press covering the casino's opening, the effort of smiling through it all seemed to be getting to him. He wore a bright blue sport coat, black slacks, a white-linen shirt, and a tie. But even his usual nattiness and his efforts to flash his creased, knowing smile could not hide his awareness that things were different out here. Invoking the name of the King of Spain at the journalists' buffet in the Monet Ballroom just a few steps from the wedding chapel would not be appropriate. A different kind of majesty reigned here. The toga-clad waitresses at Caesars Palace no doubt communicated the spirit of Julius Caesar. The pharaoh himself presided at the Luxor casino farther up the strip. The lifestyle of the doge of Venice would soon be reproduced at the Venetian, while the glory of King Arthur's court was said to be fully recaptured at the Excalibur just up Las Vegas Boulevard toward the on-ramp to Nevada 15. To mention the King of Spain in a hotel where walk-through guests could be spotted getting their pictures taken amid the marble and shiny fittings of the public bathrooms would be simply to overreach the target. Instead, Sirio did his best to mix, looked shifty, was filmed by the Bellagio's film crew in conversation with Steve Wynn, and looked toward the door. "This is quite a change for you," someone said to him. "No," he replied without bothering to force a smile, "it's quite a change for them."

Las Vegas has undergone a restaurant revolution in recent years. It's all about positioning. These aren't the old casinos with their "Midnight Chuck Wagon Buffet." These new casinos, hungry for a veneer of sophistication, have offered famous chefs and restaurateurs from around the country deals that have proved hard to turn down. The Las Vegas Convention/Visitors Authority describes it as a process where "the fantasy of food evolved into another attraction with a distinctive Las Vegas aura." Restaurant trade magazines, more blunt in their analysis, talk about the flush, relaxed foot traffic that moves nightly from casino to casino with a sense of glee previously heard only in the corporate headquarters of fast food giants.

But what is served in Las Vegas is not fast food. That would be too obvious. It is very much real food and real wine cooked and served by people who are as proud of their line of work as those in any other restaurant in the country. Standing in the marmoreal cool of the casino malls, listening to the incessant jangle of slot machines, one is impressed by these restaurants' ability to offer a satisfyingly normal experience. It is so normal, in fact, that it almost blinds one to a secondary dimension that all newly arrived restaurants in Las Vegas share.

To best understand that dimension, one should really drive out of Las Vegas, west on Nevada 15, over the crest beyond which the city disappears, and farther out on the ramrod blacktop that splits the scrub, to the massive outlet center in Primm, Nevada. Here in the blinding desert light, stripped of all context except that which a huge full parking lot can afford, one can clearly see how the principle of licensing has transformed the apparel business. Some may be here for the bargains, but most—certainly the busloads of Japanese tourists that are bused out from Las Vegas—are here for the names: the Polo player on the bathrobe, the CK on the tie, the DKNY on the blouse . . .

Apparel is one business and restaurants are another. The link between them is Pierre Cardin. Cardin made his name in haute couture. He then made his fortune by having that name put on everything from ties to underwear to nylon socks. In 1981, he bought another great name, Maxim's. One might have wanted to believe that what he was attempting would be interesting, that he was working toward a restaurant version of prêt-à-porter. In haute couture, you get detail, the fitted Balenciaga seams, the famed Fortuny pleats (the product of endless hours of work by seamstresses the French fashion world calls *les petites mains*—the little hands). In prêt-à-porter, you get much less detail but at a much more affordable price. It would have been fascinating to see Cardin take Maxim's and make an effort at creating a culinary prêt-à-porter, but that's not what Cardin wanted. He wanted culinary nylon socks. He wanted the name. "I have done all I can with Cardin. It is on everything," he obligingly told the *Wall Street Journal* in 1981. "Maxim's is a name and a name must be exploited." In due course, the name appeared on everything from orchids ($35 a stem) to evening wear and home furnishings and on the red awnings of restaurants that opened—and often closed—in cities around the world.

It is very hard to stand on the gambling floor of the Bellagio and look up at an overhead sign that has the venerable name Le Cirque alongside that for the "Race and Sports Book" (with a directional arrow pointing toward the area where one can place money on just about any sporting event occurring in the country) and come to any conclusion other than that the name is being exploited. And why shouldn't it be? Sirio was kissing hands before most of the other people exploiting their restaurant names in Las Vegas were even in culinary school. No one has put more effort into making his restaurant's name have a brand value. To understand why he'd want to do it is easy. To watch him try to do it is rather more difficult. In fact, one almost wants to look away because his heart is so not in it.

The day following the press buffet in the Monet Ballroom, after several hours of strolling in the cool of the malls that every casino sits over, I wander back to the Bellagio. On my way to the elevators that lead up to the rooms, I walk past Osteria del Circo, the restaurant that Sirio's sons have opened beside Le Cirque. Through the plateglass entrance I spot Sirio. He is standing by the door. He is looking out. There is something truly heartrending about seeing Sirio standing at the door of a restaurant not looking out at Sixty-fifth Street or Madison Avenue but toward a gambling floor crowded with people playing slot machines. Even though I'm only one of many people who have interviewed him, I am tempted to go inside and say something that a friend might say. Something reassuring, something that will get him talking about something other than his present situation, set him off on a riff about Montecatini and the King of Spain and the night Niarchos handed out the hundred-dollar bills to anyone wearing a dinner jacket. But something stops me. I don't want the desolate image that says so much about Las Vegas to dissolve in the comfortable melody of Sirio's conversational pattern, where one is both flattered to have it focused on oneself and left trying to connect the dots between the ideas. I hear it anyway in my inner ear. "People think if they have twenty-seven percent food cost and twenty-nine percent labor cost they have a restaurant," he once started. "That's not a restaurant, that's a money machine. I know. I never have an empty table in all my years. If it's slow, if there's a blizzard, for example, I take a table out. If I need a table, I put it in. I don't believe in too much space. I hate restaurants where they say, 'Is everything all right?' I'd rather say, 'Is there anything I can do for you?' That means something. If that's an espresso I'm the King of Spain. *Come si dice . . .*"

In Las Vegas, there'll be no blizzards. No frantic busboys will be sent looking for tabletops. Near panic will not reign. In Las Vegas, it's all about profiting from the foot traffic. It's all about 27 percent food cost and 29 percent labor. It's all about creating a money machine. It takes Las Vegas to make Sirio look like an idealist. An idealist in custom-made silk suits.

That same day, at six o'clock, I put on my own more humble blue suit and go to eat dinner at Le Cirque. I am greeted warmly by a hostess and led to a banquette table under the draped taffeta dome. Outside the window on the fake lake, the *jeux d'eaux* have just started and the inescapable sound of the blind Italian singer Andrea Boccelli singing the song that has become the Bellagio's theme song swells in accompaniment. At the next table, a South American mogul plays the part of a South American mogul dining at Le Cirque to perfection. He orders caviar, has his Haut-Brion decanted, talks on a cell phone, and ignores his young wife, who looks at the monkey murals similar to the ones at the original Le Cirque. There is a slight strain in the service of a restaurant just getting its legs. The half bottle of Meursault goes down easily. The ragout of rabbit with fava beans in a cream sauce served in a burnished copper casserole with accompanying spaetzle is beautiful and delicious. But something is missing. I ask the waiter where Sirio is. He smiles with relief: "He went back to New York." A few minutes later, as if to prove it, I hear him ask the mogul, "Is everything all right?"

I look toward the door. There is no danger that anyone whose presence might electrify the room will walk in. Las Vegas is the mirror image of New York in the 1940s: it has all the food and none of the names. Outside the door, people in tank tops are hollering as they press the "Bet Max" buttons on the "Blazing 7's" slot machines. Inside, the mogul has reached dessert. Here is Le Cirque Las Vegas. The waiter is serving the crème brûlée. But Sirio is gone.

⊶━━⊷

RESTAURANT
LIGHTS

To get an appetizer for the Eisner party, Chef Joachim Splichal of Patina restaurant in Los Angeles does not actually tell the young line cook working furiously at the stove that it is for the Eisner party. Nor does he say that it is for the chairman of the Walt Disney Company. Nor does he say that it is for someone at the table of a man whose driver and bodyguard—so I've been told—earlier in the day did a walk-through of the building to see how their employer would access and egress the restaurant and where his limousine would be parked while he ate. The phrase that Chef Splichal uses to drive the cook is "They're drinking Échézeaux from Jayer, make it perfect."

It is not that Splichal is unimpressed by his customer or not delighted that such a powerful and public face has chosen his restaurant; but, in a crunch, when he needs a young line cook to get an appetizer to the pass-through perfect and right now, he won't invoke the near-mythical power of a corporate identity but rather the near-mythic power of a wine-maker's name when combined with a certain slope of Burgundy's Côte de Nuits.

I am backed up against a wall in the kitchen, in a space between the coffee machine and the hot appetizer station. I have asked to be in the kitchen because I am looking for a definite moment. Something that will be truly emblematic of the restaurant business today. I'm looking for bookends. It starts at Place Gaillon in Paris. Where does it end? At moments spread over the previous two years, I have thought I've seen it. When I saw the unmistakable silhouette of Julia Child backlit by television lights as she held forth to CNN at the Aspen Food and Wine Classic, I thought that was the moment I was looking for. But with time it became one image among many. When I sat with the young women taking reservations at Nobu in New York ("We put the No into Nobu," one quipped) and watched them pore over massive reservation books timed with arrivals like an order of battle, there, too, I thought I was seeing what the restaurant business had become. But with time that became an amusing moment and no more. Now I am here, being tolerated in a crush, as I have tolerated reporters in kitchens myself. As Splichal tells his crew to start working a slew of new tables, I slip out the swinging kitchen doors into the front hallway.

Around the hostess desk, there is a crush of people. The seating plan for the evening has gotten off to a bad start. Early reservations showed up late, parties that the manager had put down as no-shows (and given their tables away) showed. Voices are being raised ever so slightly. There's the sense that the carefully monitored fifteen-minute slots that make up the reservation book are starting to pop like rivets in a doomed sub. The manager and the hostess are calm. It's just another busy night in a successful restaurant.

Knowing that I am only going to get increasingly in the way, I decide to leave. I walk out onto Melrose Avenue. Though it is dark, the sky is orange with residual smog. A limousine that I take to be Eisner's waits, with its lights off but engine running the AC, under a fluorescent streetlight. The image is desolately cold, particularly when compared to the lively bustle that I've just left. I look back at the restaurant. Is this the image I've been waiting for? Is this the American restaurant at its most emblematic: full, thriving, vital, its lights framed by the American night?

There is something about the night that restaurants need to be seen in their full dimension. It is as if only when their lights are surrounded by darkness that the meaning they hold for us becomes clear. Restaurants are shelter, welcome, companionship, and respite. The theme is old. In literature, it is in Hemingway's "A Clean Well-Lighted Place." In art, it is seen in the café tables of van Gogh's *The Café Terrace on the Place de Forum, Arles, at Night* or the people sitting in the light of the all-night coffee shop of Edward Hopper's *Nighthawks*.

But the American night that held the all-night coffee shop of that painting has changed. The coffee shop has become the gourmet coffee outlet, the lights of the Roxy have become those of the Cineplex, and the late-closing store has become the mall. The great American thoroughfare—from Fifth Avenue to Michigan Avenue to Union Square—has become a depressingly homogenized mixture of brand-name signage and megastores. In this overscaled and overdesigned urban landscape, what is the role of the restaurant?

One approach is that of the restaurant that ignores this environment, that sets itself up as its aesthetic opposite. This is the ethos of the fifteen-table restaurant started by culinary school graduates under a freeway overpass. This restaurant will not play the game. It will not be part of the "retail mix." Eating is not shopping. What restaurants offer does not come out of central shipping. Risk is involved; things can go horribly wrong or memorably right. Their lights hold a certain promise. Memories might result. The problem with this approach, laudable as it might be, is that it is essentially passive. A memorable meal may indeed be had at a small restaurant such as this, but the restaurant itself won't stop a single national retail chain from muscling in on yet another prime location.

The second approach is to compete. Not aesthetically, since there is no challenge—the smell of a stockpot or a wood-fired oven versus the smell of bubble wrap—but to compete in scale. Traditionally, the only kind of restaurants that could compete in scale with national merchandisers were fast food franchises. They had the expertise to handle the volume that was required to pay the rent. The ever-increasing appetite for good food in this country has led to the creation of a particularly American restaurant form, one that fuses the idealism of the fifteen-table restaurant under the freeway overpass with the business practices required to survive in the land of the multiplex.

In many ways, what has come to be known as "multiunit operation" evolved out of the constraints particular to the restaurant form. We are prepared (glad, in fact) to do our banking at ATMs. We visit doctors who share waiting room space (and costs). We shop at department stores that provide no service. But we don't want anyone messing with the unwritten formula that the restaurant experience requires thirty-two inches of table frontage per customer, one waiter per six tables, the possibility of three courses, and one and a half hours in which to eat them. There are, in fact, very few ways in which restaurateurs themselves can tweak the formula. Giving a waiter too many tables leads to bad service. Giving a time by which a party must vacate a table leads to charges of imperiousness. Cutting table sizes down to twenty-four inches (where's the outrage?) leads to unwanted eavesdropping, spilled wine, and generally frayed nerves. The only realistic way for a restaurateur to increase profit is to increase volume, and the only graceful way to do that is to open another restaurant.

But there is a second and more philosophical interpretation of our modern multiunit restaurant world and that is something that was almost preordained to happen since the day European gastronomy and the American market first met. The traditions of European gastronomy, with dishes such as *potage Dubarry*, the cream of cauliflower soup named after Louis XV's last paramour, implied the feeding of the elite. The American market, however, was one in which the very names of the eating establishments—tavern, roadhouse, chophouse, grill, luncheonette, pizza parlor, and Automat—implied the feeding of the masses. The fusion of both was uniquely American, as a possibility, problem, and solution, and the resolution of the seemingly incompatible principles of volume and gastronomy may, in fact, be this country's greatest contribution to the restaurant form.

Since attempting this union was nothing less than Joe Baum's life's work, it is appropriate to start the discussion of its implementation with him. Invariably wearing a double-breasted suit, with a taste for the Runyonesque (and a vocabulary to match: the wide world of spirits was reduced by him with Prohibition-era brevity to "brown" ones and "clear" ones), Joe Baum literally embodied the supremely American refusal of having one's social class be a barrier to enjoying any particular experience. In 1997, the year before he died, he invited me for a drink at the Rainbow Room on top of the GE Building in Rockefeller Center, which his company was managing at the time. (Before showing up, I stopped in at Paul Stuart to buy a hand-rolled, linen handkerchief for my breast pocket. I'd never worn one before, but I didn't want to look like a schnook, not with Joe Baum.) We sat at one of the tables in the bar and he looked south at the lights of the Empire State Building and the Chrysler Building and farther south to the World Trade Center and watching him, I said, "You've always loved skyscrapers, haven't you?" He arched his eyebrows, the way he was given to do, and said, "I love New York. To tell you the truth, I'm afraid to live anywhere else." New York represented not only the urbanity he cherished, but also held within its teeming avenues the mass density necessary for what would be the experiment of his life: how to provide a gastronomic experience not just for the few, but for the many. Skinner had his box. Mendel had his peas. Joe Baum had New York.

The main problem of serving many people at many locations simultaneously was not in providing the food and service (which had logistical solutions) but how to provide something far more abstract but just as important, a real sense of welcome. On the face of it, this would not seem like such a hard problem to solve. You simply hire someone to smile and be nice to people as they come in. This was Baum's first solution. When he managed the Newarker, he hired a woman named Frances "Fritzy" Walsh from the local Huyler's restaurant and when regulars of that restaurant came to the Newarker, she could welcome them by name. Similarly, in 1959, when RA bought Mama Leone's, they kept Gene Leone on salary for the same purpose. But such individualization of service was at odds with the volume that Baum intended to achieve and soon did. When you were operating the Four Seasons, Forum of the Twelve Caesars, La Fonda del Sol, the Brasserie, the Tower Suites, the John Peel Restaurant, Paul Revere's Tavern and Chophouse, the La Guardia Terrace Restaurant, Tavern on the Green (not to mention the concession stands at Harlem's Meer Boathouse and Brooklyn's and Manhattan's Wollman Rinks), how then did you provide a welcome? You couldn't just hope to find a perfect fit like Fritzy Walsh for each of them. You had to change the customer's expectations. Baum did just that. He didn't promote his restaurants with his own personality (or anyone else's); he promoted them by the personality of the restaurants themselves.

The RA stable of restaurants is full of examples. The "flaming wall" of chickens at La Fonda del Sol. The "traveling antipasto" at Mama Leone's. Even the famous changing seasons at the Four Seasons, when four times a year the color of everything from the staff uniforms to the ribbons used to print the menus was changed. Baum actually put his philosophy into words in 1965 in a speech before the National Restaurant Convention in Chicago when he described the creation of Zum-Zum, the rapid-service sausage counter that RA had placed in the concourse of the Pan Am Building.

"We developed a new kind of snack bar," he told the attendees. (With Baumian pride, he also told them that each stool on that snack bar did "sixty turnovers a day.") "Instead of hot dogs we'd sell them Bavarian Wurst. Instead of orange drink, we'd sell them Helle and Dunkel: light and dark beer. And if we're going to give them Bavarian Wurst, let's really give it to them. Let's make it and smoke it right there. And while we're at it, let's build smoke ovens so they see it being smoked. Let them see it come out of the oven at 11:00 A.M. and right into the rye roll. (Remember, we want a dime or fifteen cents more for these sausages. . . . Make them worth it.) Design the place to look like a sausage shop, ice-box wood, and white-tile walls and immaculate. Let's hang those sausages all over the place. Let their mouths water. Give it a name that sounds right and suggests speed. Zum-Zum. The whole place becomes a sign."

In a single description of a sausage counter (admittedly one by way of someone with an eye for detail and design like Joe Baum), there is the description of what for Baum and RA would always be the solution to the problem of providing a welcome at many different locations simultaneously: let the restaurant be what attracts the customer. It was a very American solution, one that had long been practiced in hot dog stands shaped like hot dogs, Automats that delighted children and adults, and burger joints where the curbside service was provided by waitresses on roller skates. But it had never before been applied—not on a multiunit scale—to gastronomy.

Baum's ideological heirs might be said to be Lettuce Entertain You Enterprises (LEYE), whose founder, Richard Melman, is the dominant force on the Chicago restaurant scene. Tellingly, it is Joe Baum's longtime partner, Michael Whiteman, who has perhaps described the

LEYE methodology best. In the restaurant trade book *Restaurants That Work*, he is quoted as saying that Melman "has created better than anybody in the last two decades, a concept for a 'narrative' restaurant. Richard's restaurants tell a story. [He has] made up a fictional story, in his office, with his designers and they built the restaurants around the story."

The night before my scheduled interview with Melman, I joined the crowds strolling around Chicago's River North. This is a central section of the city that twenty years earlier had been filled with empty warehouses and today is a thriving neighborhood of art galleries, hotels, and restaurants, a particularly rich cluster of them being LEYE properties. Within a few blocks of each other, I got to see restaurants with such perfected "narratives" as Maggiano's Little Italy, with its family-sized portions; Ben Pao Restaurant and Satay Bar, with its lacquered wood and opium-den feel; Shaw's Crab House, with its trays of iced shellfish; Brasserie Jo, with its La Coupole–like proportions; and Papagus Greek Taverna, which had managed to re-create a Greek village's café terrace, complete with white walls and blue tables and chairs, right on the pavement of 620 North State. The next morning, I gave the taxi driver the address of the corporate offices from which all these concepts emanated and I was driven far from River North, along Lake Michigan for a few miles. Sheridan Road is an unimposing traffic artery and I was deposited in front of a squat red-brick building whose other tenants included dental groups and travel agents.

The receptionist (sitting in front of a large mural of an iceberg lettuce) informed me that "Rich" was just then taking a meeting and kindly offered to get me a cup of coffee while I waited. I sipped at the coffee and leafed through some of the restaurant trade magazines on the table in front of me. In this world, ideas are "rolled out," failures are "reconcepted," successes are "chained," and frozen vegetables are advertised for their "plate coverage" qualities. One can get a very utilitarian idea of the restaurant business from reading these magazines and it is perhaps because of that that I started thinking about what precisely I had seen in River North the night before.

I hadn't seen mom-and-pop restaurants. I had seen restaurants designed to look like mom-and-pop restaurants. It is a sort of ersatz experience that is often called "Disneyfied." What the word is intended to convey is a retail environment with a strong entertainment component and a veneer of good cheer. Times Square is often cited as an example because of Disney's vision for the formerly seedy section of Manhattan. The word, however, has been applied to cities for a long time, much longer than the Disney Company's actual interest in Times Square. An early sighting of the word occurs in Thomas Pynchon's 1966 essay for the New York Times Magazine, "A Journey into the Mind of Watts," written about the Los Angeles neighborhood that had burned in race riots the previous year. "Yet in the daytime's brilliance and heat," wrote Pynchon, "it is hard to believe there is any mystery to Watts. Everything seems out in the open, all of it real, no plastic faces, no transistors, no Muzak, or Disneyfied landscaping or smiling little chick to show you around. Not in Raceriotland." What is being juxtaposed here is indeed the spurious and the genuine; but also, it would seem, two conflicting urban visions: "Disneyfied landscaping" (infantilized order) and "Raceriotland" (urban blight). Either principle could have been applied to River North. By the mid-seventies, the area's dilapidated warehouses risked receiving not the Disneyfied solution but the parking lot solution in which great tracts of it would be razed and paved. It wasn't. The restaurants I'd seen the previous night may have had the sheen and wattage that marked them as coming straight from a designer's table, but it was those very same restaurants that saved the neighborhood.

A full hour had transpired now and there had been much smiling back and forth between the receptionist and me. She finally was able to tell me that Rich could fit me in now, between the meeting that was about to end and another one that was scheduled to start, and she led me into his office as two men carrying legal pads covered in notes came out.

Melman had carefully maintained over-the-shoulder hair and wore pressed slacks and a summer-weight denim shirt. We shook hands and he apologized for keeping me waiting. He sat back down behind his desk and I sat in a leather chair across from him with my own legal pad at the ready. He started by talking about his first restaurant, R. J. Grunts, that he opened near Lincoln Park in 1971. "I wanted a place where I could listen to James Taylor, not Muzak," he said. "I wanted the atmosphere to be like one of those hippie cafés that existed at the time where you could sit all night without being bothered but one that was run professionally enough so that you could have dinner there and still make an eight o'clock movie." We'd spoken for about ten minutes more when he looked down at his watch. The fact that he'd looked down at his watch while he spoke seemed to bother him.

"I know you have another meeting scheduled," I said to help him out of his embarrassment.

He nodded that this was indeed the case and gave me his home phone number and told me to call him and he started to get up. Then the lack of time actually helped me. He knew I'd come a long way to talk about multiunit restaurants and he didn't want me to leave with nothing. But there was no time for a broad-ranging discussion on the subject. "Look," he said, stopping as he led me toward the door. "I'm going to tell you something I don't usually tell journalists. The ideal restaurant is one product, one employee and two hundred customers."

"That's a hot dog stand."

"Exactly. Now take that concept and times it by the amount of items you make, times it by the number of people working there, times it by the amount of customers you serve, times it by the quality you're trying to do, times it by the number of restaurants you have . . ." He trailed off and looked inquiringly at me. Did I get it? I thought so. You take a hot dog stand and introduce an indefinite number of variables. At the point where the greatest number of things can go wrong, it becomes a restaurant. A restaurant is a hot dog stand doing a high-wire act.

The analogy I suspect would please Danny Meyer, the founder of the Union Square Hospitality Group in New York. He has an open smile and a ready laugh that hint at his midwestern roots. He grew up in Saint Louis in a household that seemed to fuse ideal aspects of two continents. His father, an organizer of customized tours of Europe, always had a bottle of Beaujolais-Villages on the dinner table, and the family's high-strung French poodle was named Ratatouille; but at night young Danny would lie in bed listening to the Saint Louis Cardinals' games being called on KMOX. (His eyes still brighten when he recalls seeing Stan Musial's final season or the time pitcher Bob Gibson got two outs even though his leg had just been broken by a Roberto Clemente line drive.) After studying political science at Trinity College in Hartford, Connecticut, he moved to New York, where for a brief period he sold store security devices, then he worked as a cook, and finally he became a manager at the downtown restaurant Pesca. In 1985, at the age of twenty-seven, he opened Union Square Cafe.

"I'm in the walls over there," he says, fondly remembering the restaurant he ran for nine years before opening his second restaurant, Gramercy Tavern on East Twentieth Street, in 1994. Since then, he has opened two more: Tabla, a revisionist Indian restaurant, and Eleven Madison Park, which, with its floor-to-ceiling leaded windows and the ornate plasterwork of the Cass Gilbert New York Life Building (itself built on the site of the original Madison Square Garden), has managed to render perfectly in a restaurant both a historical sense and a modern sensibility. The restaurants demarcate a certain downtown territory, and in the process of opening them, Danny has found himself faced with the same problems that faced Joe Baum. The truly successful mastery of volume isn't about logistics but about welcome. How do you maintain the level of welcome and service you've become known for in newer restaurants where you're not at the door, never mind "in the walls"?

With four restaurants at the time of writing, it is an important question for him. He can't be at the door of all of them or taking orders or cooking the food, but he can make sure that the people who are doing it know how he would do it if he were. The way he does this is he buses his own table. We have sat at a corner table at the bar of Eleven Madison Park for over an hour. He has told me that it was an honor for him when Joe Baum would come to eat at Gramercy Tavern. He has told me that opening a restaurant today has "the production costs of a Broadway show." He has described his corporate philosophy as one of "enlightened hospitality," which is based on "taking care of the customer and taking care of each other." It all sounds vaguely New Age until he proves what he means. Toward the end of the conversation, after he's suggested that I walk around his restaurants with him, he picks up his empty cup and saucer. I follow his example and we walk through the swinging kitchen doors to the dishwashing area where we place cups, saucers, and spoons into the appropriate containers that will later be slid into the machines. He has four restaurants, hundreds of employees—many whose job is precisely to bus tables—and he buses his own table. He is not trying to create an "atmosphere" in his restaurants—something that any designer can create with enough low ceilings and hard surfaces to bounce the decibels around—he is trying to increase the degree of difficulty of the Baumian philosophy. It was Joe Baum's genius to be able to take the restaurateur's persona out of the restaurant's personality; Danny Meyer is keeping the scale but putting the personality back.

It is done through communication. To walk through Danny Meyer's restaurants in the moments before they open for business is to momentarily think that one has taken a wrong turn and stumbled into a human communication workshop. At Eleven Madison Park, the cooks sit on a banquette in the dining room and give a waiter who has just been promoted a round of applause. ("First time I've seen that," I say. Danny nods proudly.) Upstairs at Tabla, a young black manager wearing a spread-collar shirt and, his jacket off, displaying silk suspenders stands before his attentive floor staff listing a few things he's seen done wrong in the previous service and wants rectified. "Come on," he says, football-coach style, "we can do better." Danny stands back, unobtrusively listening. Then we go downstairs to the bar. We talk for a few minutes about how well beer goes with Indian food. He points to a design motif running along the bar. "It's similar to a tabla drum," he says and smiles, "but not too much. I didn't want to over-theme." Then he spots the manager coming down the stairs from the staff meeting and walks over to him with his hand outstretched. "I salute your passion," he says.

"Thank you, Danny," the young man says, clearly appreciating the words. Then he turns to the reservation book and starts to block out the dining room for the night.

Our interview is over and I get my coat and say good-bye to Danny and for a moment I stand outside the restaurant. The last rays of a weak winter sun shine through the bare branches of the plane trees of Madison Park. Beyond the dog run is the Flatiron Building, immortalized in its fogbound splendor in Alfred Stieglitz's famed 1902 photograph.

A restaurateur with a weaker stomach for risk would have been unable to resist making "Old New York" the restaurant's theme. But though the restaurant's name is written in gold-leaf stenciling on the windows, and there are a few old sepia photographs of the neighborhood along the restaurant's corridors, it is clear that this was not his intention. No overtheming. Said with a smile but meant seriously. Danny Meyer is doing something else. He is attempting the hardest trick that a hot dog stand on a high wire can perform. He is creating theme restaurants where the theme is service. He knows that cannot be achieved simply by putting up mission statements in the staff changing rooms. To do that, he must morph his personality into each one of his employees. That is why he salutes your passion. That is why he buses his table.

After leaving Danny, I wrapped my coat about myself and started up Madison Avenue. It was rush hour and the streets were teeming. Livery service cars waited for their clients outside the better office buildings and people carrying packages ran toward Federal Express offices to make the last pickup. I did not walk quickly. I knew where I was headed. When I was in New York, it had become a habit of mine to end days of interviews walking toward 5 East Fifty-fifth Street. It was the original location of Le Pavillon and had become for me something of a beacon, the walk there a way of going over conversations I'd had during the day. Tonight, as I walked through the crowded streets, I found myself thinking, as I often did, of Soulé.

The modern restaurant world would surely have left him mystified. His idea of creating "a narrative" was to put up a mural of the bay of St. Jean-de-Luz in La Côte Basque. To communicate his values to his staff he locked them out. The 1945 strike had been about the money the waiters wanted to make. The 1960 walkout by Pierre Franey about cutting costs. By the time of the 1962 lockout, it was simply about principles.

On January 26, 1962, Craig Claiborne informed his readers that Soulé had the following notice distributed to all departments at La Côte Basque. "Due to insubordination by the dining room crew of orders issued by me, I have no alternative but to close the restaurant as of tonight until such a time that my orders will be complied with." The man whose withering look, it was said, could curdle a béarnaise was now pitted against the Dining Room Employees' Local, whose views of providing *le standing* did not include the sacrifices Soulé knew to be necessary. Being Soulé, the stage where his orders were complied with was not quickly reached. Before he would stand for insubordination, he would sell the restaurant. That is precisely what he did. The restaurateur who bought it was unable to make it a success and in 1965, clearly satisfied that he'd made his point, Soulé took it back. But it was not the same.

Truman Capote's unfinished novel *Answered Prayers* paints the scene well in the elegiac last paragraph of the chapter entitled "La Côte Basque 1965." "Although the priest and the assassin were still whispering and sipping at their table," Capote wrote, "the restaurant's rooms had emptied, M. Soulé had retired. Only the hatcheck girl and a few waiters impatiently flicking napkins remained. Stewards were resetting the tables, sprucing the flowers for the evening visitors. It was an atmosphere of luxurious exhaustion, like a ripened, shedding rose, while all that waited outside was the failing New York afternoon."

There is a melancholic air to the paragraph, an autumnal sadness due in part to the image of the shedding rose, the fading afternoon light, and the suspicion that the wine is wearing off. But in Capote's light brushwork, there is the sense that Soulé has not only "retired" (to his changing room, to change his suit, as he always did before going out on the street) but is also somehow diminished. The challenges that twenty-five years of running the best French restaurant in America have faced him with have taken their toll. He may have thought of the credit card and Harry Cohn and the charges of anti-Semitism and the Kennedy walkout and the threat that the "four-flushers" represented as individual challenges to overcome. He may have failed to see the pattern. In a life contained between his upper Park Avenue apartment and his two Upper East Side restaurants, he may very well not even have realized that it wasn't the Dining Room Employees' Local that had changed, but the country.

On a cold January day in 1966, in a country where the government was engaged in the war on poverty and several U.S. senators were unsuccessfully attempting to halt the resumption of bombing in North Vietnam; on a day in which an early dusting of snow had given way to a bitter cold; between lunch and dinner services, in the bathroom of La Côte Basque, Henri Soulé suffered a heart attack and died. One of the waiters ran out into the winter dusk and through the afternoon crowds and ran across Fifth Avenue and down Fifty-fifth Street and into La Caravelle, where he knew he would find some of Soulé's ex-employees—"the busboys from the west side"—and, entering, he shouted, *"Le patron est mort!"* The boss is dead.

There is a sad symmetry to the fact that it was 1966, the year that Alice Waters would turn to cooking, in essence the year that the United States had reached the stage in which, out of its own history, it had produced the conditions that would finally liberate French food from all the stultified rules of *le standing*. That someone could put *brandade de morue* on a menu without fear that it wouldn't be considered a good restaurant.

Soulé would never have admitted that America could influence either him or French cooking. He was too formed when he arrived. The country could not teach him anything. All it could do was learn. Throughout Soulé's career, there was an almost antagonistic relationship with his adopted country, one that was made even more pronounced by the fact that following his death, there was no American funeral service for him.

"The body of Henri Soulé proprietor of Le Pavillon and La Côte Basque, will be at the Universal Funeral Chapel at Lexington Avenue and 52nd Street until 2 P.M. today. There will be no funeral ser-

vice here for the restaurateur, who died of a heart attack Thursday afternoon at La Côte Basque. The body will be taken to France, where
funeral arrangements will be made by his family." One reads this tiny
notice in the *Times* (which appeared the day following his much larger
obituary) and finds oneself trying to fill it out with some sort of
meaning. Not even a service! Why? Did those immediately responsible for the arrangement sense that it would not be as glorious as he
would have wished, that fickleness would get the better of all the
great names who had once been so eager to be smiled at and sat but
now would not show up? That all the snubs he'd delivered would be
returned? That the only people who would fill the seats at this, the
last room he would seat, would be the members of his staff, with
whom he'd fought for so long but for whom he was still *le patron*?

Or was it more profound? Did it point to the distance between two countries that Soulé had never bridged? Did those responsible for the arrangements realize that there was no point in
pretending otherwise? This man, who had reached such a level of
renown that J. Edgar Hoover himself, a good customer, had presented
him with a porcelain ashtray on which were reproduced the thumb-
prints he'd given the immigration authorities on the day of his arrival,
was returning to France as unchanged by America as on the spring day
in 1939 when the funnel colors of the *Normandie* appeared in the passage between Staten Island and Brooklyn known as the Narrows,
which marks the entrance to New York Harbor.

I had reached Fifth Avenue and Fifty-fifth Street. The fact that
this intersection marked the original location of Le Pavillon was not
the only reason that I often headed here. The southwestern quadrant
of the intersection also marked the location of what had been the
Gotham Hotel, the place where the luncheon for my grandfather's
send-off to Europe had been held in 1956. The luncheon over, they
had sailed to Europe aboard the *Rome*. My father, who had left for Eu-

rope four years before to write poetry, met the ship in Naples. Together (with a French poodle named Roodle) they spent six months
driving around Italy, France, and Spain in a large black Citroën. When
the trip ended, my grandparents came back to New York. But my father stayed, eventually moved to Spain, and several years later I was
born. Fifth Avenue at Fifty-fifth Street was thus not only the place
where Soulé had first gone into business in America but, more personally, also the place where my family's European journey might be
said to have begun.

As I always did, I stood on the eastern side of the intersection. The Gotham was now the Peninsula, and in its transformation
had become much more elegant. The St. Regis Hotel—facing it across
Fifth Avenue—had not changed much. The building itself was still ma-
jestically Edwardian and the doormen in their top hats and capelike
coats stood outside whistling for cabs with the same firmness that
they always must have shown. Five East Fifty-fifth Street, however,
had changed. The address, which had once been that of Le Pavillon
and then La Côte Basque; which had been, in essence, the proudest
restaurant address in the United States, was now the Disney Store. I
stood before its lit-up windows looking in at the tourists buying the
assorted merchandise that the store sells. At a different moment, seeing this happening in what had once been Soulé's very "sanctuary"
may have said something to me about the changes New York City has
undergone. But I was thinking of something else. I was still thinking
of Soulé's body going back to France. To understand the extent to
which he'd been un-Americanized was one thing, to go about achieving what he could not was another. How did one do it? What was the
process by which one became closer to a country? The process that
Soulé would not or could not look for; the one he certainly never
found?

Because I arrived in this country with little more than my
cooking knives, I had felt particularly close to a generation of chefs

who went through the process before me. At La Caravelle, Roger Fessaguet had sat with me recalling some of his story. On the lapel of his
suit, he wore the green ribbon of the Ordre de Mérite Agricole discreetly superimposed over the red one of the Légion d'Honneur, both
given to him by the French government for his services to French
cooking in the United States. As is often the case with this generation
of chefs, the subject he warmed to was not his honors but a time long
before he received them when he was a fresh-faced seventeen-year-
old in 1949 and he'd just arrived in Baltimore Harbor aboard a Liberty
Ship. These were the ships that the U.S. government sent over to Eu
rope loaded with materials for the postwar reconstruction. They went
over full, but they always came back empty. To give them ballast during the crossing of the Atlantic, their holds were often filled with
sand. On the ship that Monsieur Fessaguet crossed on, some grain had
gotten mixed in with the sand. "When they opened the holds in Baltimore," he told me, "the wheat had sprouted." Here was an image
that captured the journey of French food in this country, not Soulé's
body being flown back to France. But a living image. A field of France
floating on Baltimore Harbor.

When one has felt the pull of two continents, such images
become dear to one. They are not the rah-rah oath of allegiance stuff
that, dear as citizenship is, so oversimplifies the process of belonging.
Months later, I saw it even more vividly on Gardiners Bay in East
Hampton, Long Island, when Chef Jean Vergnes, who had served his
apprenticeship in Grenoble in the 1930s but whom I was interviewing
about his jobs as chef of the Colony and later Le Cirque, stopped in
midsentence, pointed at a boy running along the beach before us, and
said, "That's Pierre Franey's grandson." His friend, Pierre Franey, with
whom he used to play pétanque on the narrow road outside, had died
the year before. In that moment, I realized that the journey that began
by embarking on the *Normandie* in 1939 had a living legacy, one that
was right here before me in an American boy running along an Amer-

ican beach. A process did take place, however improbable it might at times appear.

I'd felt it myself soon after in the moments preceding the birth of my son. It had been thirteen years since I'd stood embarrassed in a New York grocery store looking down at a handful of coins, unable to make 65 cents' change automatically because I didn't know which coins were worth 25 cents and which where worth 10 and 5. As it was for so many others, restaurants had been my way into the country, their din and rituals a place I felt I belonged. Standing in the hospital corridor, I happened to glance out the window at the palm tops and Hollywood Hills shrouded in a predawn mist. I'd understood then that after all the kitchens in whose afternoon silence I'd prepped, all the services I'd felt ignite as the orders started coming in, all the ranges I'd stepped away from hours later with my head still filled with cooking temperatures, and all the American nights I'd stepped exhaustedly out into, for the first time I would actually have a stake in the country. As I held my wife's hand and she was wheeled into the delivery room, I knew I no longer had to keep finding a home in restaurants. I was ready to start my own.

A shrill whistle for a cab from one of the doormen of the St. Regis brought me out of my reverie and I realized that I must have been standing there for a long time because the Disney Store was now closed for the night. I knew this was the moment I'd been looking for. I was saying good-bye to a generation of restaurant workers in whom I'd seen my own journey reflected. I brushed the door that had been Le Pavillon's service entrance once for good luck and started down Fifty-fifth Street. It was cold and it was time to find somewhere warm. It was time to find someplace to eat.

⬦

SELECTED BIBLIOGRAPHY

Batterberry, Michael, and Ariane Batterberry. *On the Town in New York*. New York: Scribner, 1973.

Beard, James. *Delights and Prejudices*. New York: Atheneum, 1964.

——. *James Beard's American Cookery*. Boston: Little, Brown, 1972.

——. *Beard on Food*. New York: Alfred A. Knopf, 1974.

——. *Love and Kisses and a Halo of Truffles: Letters to Helen Evans Brown*. Ed. John Ferrone. New York: Arcade Publishing, 1994.

Beebe, Lucius. *The Big Spenders*. New York: Doubleday, 1966.

——. *Lucius Beebe Reader, The*. New York: Doubleday, 1967.

Behr, Edward. *Prohibition*. New York: Arcade Publishing, 1996.

Bemelmans, Ludwig. *La Bonne Table*. New York: Simon and Schuster, 1964.

Birmingham, Stephen. *Our Crowd: The Great Jewish Families of New York*. New York: Harper & Row, 1967.

Brody, Iles. *The Colony*. New York: Greenberg, 1945.

Bugialli, Giuliano. *The Fine Art of Italian Cooking*. New York: Times Books, 1977.

Chamberlain, Samuel. *Italian Bouquet: An Epicurean Tour of Italy*. New York: Gourmet, 1958.

Child, Julia, Louisette Bertholle, and Simone Beck. *Mastering the Art of French Cooking*. New York: Alfred A. Knopf, 1961.

Claiborne, Craig. *A Feast Made for Laughter*. New York: Doubleday, 1982.

Clark, Robert. *James Beard: A Biography*. New York: HarperCollins, 1993.

David, Elizabeth. *A Book of Mediterranean Food*. London: Lehman, 1950.

———. *French Country Cooking*. London: Lehman, 1951.

———. *Italian Food*. London: Macdonald and Co., 1954.

———. *French Provincial Cooking*. London: Michael Joseph, 1960.

Erenberg, Lewis. *Steppin' Out: New York Nightlife and the Transformation of American Culture*. Westport, Connecticut: Greenwood Press, 1981.

Escoffier, Auguste. *Memories of My Life*. Trans. Laurence Escoffier. New York: Van Nostrand Reinhold, 1997.

Fisher, M. F. K. *The Gastronomical Me*. New York: Duell, Sloan and Pearce, 1943.

———. *Map of Another Town: A Memoir of Provence*. Boston: Little, Brown, 1964.

———. *Stay Me, Oh Comfort Me: Journals and Stories 1933–1941*. New York: Pantheon, 1993.

———. *Last House: Reflections, Dreams and Observations 1943–1991*. New York: Pantheon, 1995.

———. *A Life in Letters: Correspondence 1929–1991*. Ed. Norah K. Barr, Marsha Moran, and Patrick Moran. Washington: Counterpoint, 1997.

Franey, Pierre, Richard Flaste, and Bryan Miller. *A Chef's Tale*. New York: Alfred A. Knopf, 1994.

Gitlin, Todd. *The Sixties: Years of Hope, Days of Rage*. New York: Bantam, 1987.

Greene, Gael. *Bite: A New York Restaurant Strategy*. New York: W. W. Norton, 1971.

Grossman, Peter. *American Express: The Unofficial History of the People Who Built the Great Financial Empire*. New York: Crown, 1987.

Guillot, André. *La Grande Cuisine Bourgeoise*. Paris: Flammarion, 1976.

Hale, Dennis, and Jonathan Eisen, eds. *The California Dream*. New York: Macmillan, 1968.

Hazan, Marcella. *The Classic Italian Cookbook*. New York: Harper's Magazine Press, 1973.

Hibben, Sheila. *American Regional Cookery*. Boston: Little, Brown, 1946.

Jones, Evan. *American Food: The Gastronomic Story*. New York: E. P. Dutton, 1975.

———. *Epicurean Delight: The Life and Times of James Beard*. New York: Alfred A. Knopf, 1990.

Jullian, Philippe. *Edward and the Edwardians*. New York: Viking, 1967.

Lang, George. *Nobody Knows the Truffles I've Seen*. New York: Alfred A. Knopf, 1998.

Marcuse, Herbert. *An Essay on Liberation*. Boston: Beacon Press, 1969.

Mariani, John. *America Eats Out*. New York: Morrow, 1991.

Markarian, Yervand. *Kavkaz*. N.p., 1996.

Maxtone-Graham, John. *The Only Way to Cross*. New York: Macmillan, 1972.

McWilliams, Carey. *Factories in the Fields: The Story of Migratory Farm Labor in California*. Boston: Little, Brown, 1939.

Michaels, Leonard, David Reid, and Raquel Scherr, eds. *West of the West: Imagining California*. San Francisco: North Point Press, 1989.

Morris, Jan. *Manhattan '45*. New York: Oxford University Press, 1987.

Morton, Frederick. *The Rothschilds: A Family Portrait*. New York: Atheneum, 1962.

Muscatine, Doris, Maynard A. Amerine, and Bob Thompson, eds. *The University of California Sotheby Book of California Wine*. Berkeley: University of California Press, 1984.

Olney, Richard. *The French Menu Cookbook*. New York: Simon and Schuster, 1970.

———. *Simple French Food*. New York: Atheneum, 1974.

———. *Reflexions*. New York: Brick Tower Press, 1999.

Pejsa, Jane. *Romanoff, Prince of Rogues: The Life and Times of a Hollywood Icon*. Minneapolis: Kenwood Publishing, 1997.

Pellegrini, Angelo. *The Unprejudiced Palate*. New York: Macmillan, 1952.

Reichl, Ruth. *Tender at the Bone: Growing Up at the Table*. New York: Random House, 1998.

Root, Waverley. *The Food of France*. New York: Alfred A. Knopf, 1958.

———. *The Food of Italy*. New York: Atheneum, 1971.

Schoonmaker, Frank, and Tom Marvel. *American Wines*. New York: Duell, Sloan and Pearce, 1941.

Starr, Kevin. *Endangered Dreams: The Great Depression in California*. New York: Oxford University Press, 1996.

Sussman, Warren. *Culture as History: The Transformation of American Society in the Twentieth Century*. New York: Pantheon, 1984.

Veblen, Thorstein. *The Theory of the Leisure Class*. New York: Macmillan, 1899.

Vergnes, Jean. *A Seasoned Chef*. New York: Donald I. Fine, 1987.

Wechsberg, Joseph. *Blue Trout and Black Truffles: The Peregrinations of an Epicure*. New York: Alfred A. Knopf, 1953.

———. *Dining at the Pavillon*. Boston: Little, Brown, 1962.

———. *First Time Around, The*. Boston: Little, Brown, 1970.

INDEX

strikes:
  agriculture and, 141–42
  Le Pavillon and, 91–92, 191
Suarez, Justino, 118
Summer Cooking (David), 107
Surmain, André, 75, 84–89
Swallow, 201
Swanson Frozen Dinners, 88–89

Tabla, 221, 223
Tavern on the Green, 162, 216
Tchelistcheff, André, 143
television, 173
  Child and, 43, 99, 212
Terrail, Patrick, 165, 167
The Colony, *see* Colony, The
Thélin, Aimé, 37
theme restaurants, 60, 218
Thomas, Gregory, 98
Time, 93
Titze, Theodore, 30–31
Tosca, 152, 154–55
Tower, Jeremiah, 133, 135, 148, 153–54,
    156, 163
  career of, 149–52
  influences on, 146, 160
  menus written by, 136–37
Tower Suites, 216
Troisgros, 40, 197
Trumps, 164
"21" Club, 5, 10, 25–28, 31, 49, 61, 79, 85,
    86, 103, 193

Union Square Cafe, 221
Unprejudiced Palate, The (Pellegrini),
    181

Vatel Club, 92–93
Verdon, René, 94–95, 117
Vergnes, Jean, 191, 192, 229

volume, 53–54, 217, 222
  exclusivity versus, 214–15

W, 193
waiters, 5, 57, 69, 70, 74, 123, 147–48,
    214, 224
  Russian service and, 32, 92, 106, 189
Wall Street Journal, 208
Walsh, Frances "Fritzy," 216
Waters, Alice, 4, 118, 121–22, 132, 133, 135,
    148, 149–50, 154, 156, 162–63, 168,
    171, 202, 226
  influences on, 126–33
Waxman, Jonathan, 163
Wechsberg, Joseph, 37–41, 53, 65–66,
    76, 77, 78, 81–82, 126
Wechsler, Abraham, 54–55
Weiss, Walter, 26
Whalen, Grover A., 8, 10, 12
Whiteman, Michael, 217–18
Windows on the World, 1, 166, 195
Windsor, Duke and Duchess of, 16, 18,
    77, 188
wine business, 4, 78–84, 166, 193
  California and, 142–46, 147, 162
Winiarski, Warren, 143
Wolfert, Paula, 180
Wolfgang Puck Cafés, 175–76
women, 4, 177–78
  as chefs, 62–63
  see also specific women
Women's Wear Daily, 193
World's Fair (1939), French Pavilion at,
    3–4, 7–12, 15, 112, 164, 173
Wynn, Steve, 205, 206

Zagat, Nina, 199
Zagat, Tim, 199
Zagat Survey, 199–200, 204
Zelayeta, Elena, 62–63
Zum-Zum, 51, 217